W9-DAV-532

The stone portico pictured on the cover was the entrance to the Frederick W. Stone farm house where the first OAC classes were held. The original farm became part of the first Johnston Hall, which was torn down in 1928 and replaced by the present building. The portico now stands on the edge of Johnston Green.

Hatching the Cowbird's Egg
The Creation of the University of Guelph

David R. Murray

ISBN   0-88955-169-3

1. University of Guelph - History.   2. Education, Higher - Ontario - History.   3. Universities and colleges - Ontario - History.   I. Title.

Hatching the Cowbird's Egg: The Creation of the University of Guelph

© University of Guelph and David R. Murray, 1989
All rights reserved, including right of reproduction in whole or in part in any form or storage medium without permission of the author or the University of Guelph.
Published by the University of Guelph in recognition of the university's twenty-fifth anniversary, with support from the twenty-fifth anniversary committee, chaired by Earl MacNaughton.

Cover design: Theresa Leyes
Inside drawings: Erich Barth, Gordon Couling and Marlene Jofriet.

Printed and bound in Canada.

*Dedicated to the memory of John Bell,
University of Guelph classics professor and chair of the
Department of Languages and Literatures (1980-87),
a source of inspiration to his students and colleagues.*

Table of Contents

Preface

I am grateful to many people whose help has made this book possible. Earl MacNaughton and the members of the 25th Anniversary Committee of the University of Guelph have been most encouraging and supportive from the beginning. Two presidents of the University of Guelph, Burton C. Matthews and Brian Segal, have each read the manuscript and given their support. Clayton Switzer, former deputy minister of agriculture and food, granted me access to the ministry papers held by the Public Archives of Ontario. Alan Adlington, then deputy minister of colleges and universities, granted me access to the ministry records.

A number of colleagues read parts or all of the manuscript in draft form and many made helpful suggestions. I express my thanks to each of them — Terence Crowley, Jim Stevens, Trevor Lloyd Jones, Donald A. Barnum, John Gilman, Blair Neatby, M.H.M MacKinnon, Gilbert Stelter and Leonard Conolly.

Alix McEwen of the Public Archives of Ontario helped me with research at a critical point, and the changes she suggested made this a better book. I am also indebted to numerous other staff members of the Public Archives of Ontario who facilitated my research and were always cheerfully willing to help. Nancy Sadek and her staff at the University of Guelph archives never failed in finding what I needed and always at short notice. Ruth Mickus and Joyce Doyle expertly typed and re-typed drafts of the manuscript for me. In this, as in so many other things, their assistance has been invaluable. Ann Middleton of the University of Guelph's Public Relations and Information Department edited the manuscript with great care and Dorothy Hadfield typeset the book.

I have relied on information supplied by a number of people who agreed to be interviewed or who supplied material on their role in the creation of the university. Sadly, J.D. MacLachlan, the first president of the University of Guelph, died before the book was completed, but

I am indebted to him and to those listed below for sharing their recollections with me: Trevor Lloyd Jones, Aubrey Hagar, William Stewart, J.R. McCarthy, Everett Biggs, Tom McEwan, Fred Presant, N.R. Richards, Ralph Campbell, John Gilman, Don Barnum and Jim Stevens.

I am solely responsible for the content of the book and for any errors or omissions it may contain. I am pleased to dedicate it to the faculty, staff, students and alumni who have worked to make the University of Guelph the distinguished institution it is today and especially to the memory of John Bell who exemplified a selfless commitment to excellence in teaching, scholarship and service to the community.

David Murray,
Guelph, May, 1989.

Hatching the Cowbird's Egg

Introduction

The creation of the University of Guelph in 1964 has many of the elements of a mystery story. Although the idea was not new, no one could have predicted the sequence of events surrounding the metamorphosis of three colleges into a university. Confusion exists about who was actually responsible for creating the university and who designed its key features. This book attempts to unravel the major elements of the mystery and to outline the roles played by the various protagonists.

The outcome of the mystery might best be described as a happy accident. It was, in part, the culmination of a long campaign by alumni of the three Department of Agriculture colleges — Ontario Agricultural College (OAC), Ontario Veterinary College (OVC) and Macdonald Institute. OAC alumni, in particular, wished to see their institution raised to university status. Premier John Robarts pragmatically recognized that Guelph could quickly and inexpensively be adapted to accommodate a large number of university students. With the explosive demand for university places looming, the government required inexpensive and practical solutions of the kind Guelph offered.

We may tend to think that historical events follow some fixed and pre-ordained plan. They do not. The University of Guelph did not come into existence in 1964 as part of a carefully developed and long-thought-out strategy. Instead, a confluence of circumstances fortuitously occurred in the two years 1962-64 and paved the way for the emergence of Guelph as a university.

The transformation might have occurred much earlier. Legislative proposals for a university at Guelph go back to 1945. It was equally possible that university status could have been rejected altogether by the Ontario government, which had complete control over the colleges through the Department of Agriculture. Had this happened, the three colleges would have evolved very differently, either continuing their association with the University of Toronto or perhaps following European patterns as technical institutes.

If university status had been achieved before 1964, Guelph might have been a very different institution from what it is today. Plans in the 1950s, and as late as 1963, called for a state university, controlled by and accountable to the minister of agriculture, not an autonomous university governed by a board of governors in a similar fashion to other Ontario universities. The struggle to achieve university status at Guelph was also a struggle that determined the shape the future university would take. In the end, the timing of the decision to grant university status turned out to be a significant element in determining the academic shape of the University of Guelph. The idea of a state university, closely tied to the Department of Agriculture, was rejected in favour of an institution that fitted into the existing pattern of Ontario university development.

Because OAC, OVC and Macdonald Institute had been under the direct control of the Department of Agriculture, the government of Ontario acted as midwife in the birth of the University of Guelph. Indeed, without government approval, no change could have taken place. But because of the vital connection of the colleges to the agricultural life of the province and the prominent political support rural Ontario offered to the ruling Conservative party, the efforts to transform the Guelph colleges took on a byzantine complexity.

The story of how the University of Guelph came into being is a tale of alumni dedication and the unremitting efforts of Dr. J.D. MacLachlan, president of the Ontario Agricultural College and later of the Federated Colleges. It is also a chronicle of government policy on higher education and agricultural education and research in the late 1950s and 1960s.

When it came, the change was dramatic in its suddenness and traumatic in its effect. OAC had existed for ninety years as part of a government department, its faculty and staff belonging to Ontario's civil service and working in a civil service atmosphere that included signing in for work in the morning and signing out in the evening. The two colleges that joined OAC in the 20th century were part of the same atmosphere. Both the sudden break from government control and the rapid influx of students in the arts and sciences meant difficult adjustments for a campus accustomed to rural conservatism.

The University of Guelph emerged from a process in which the Ontario government relinquished control over its agricultural and veterinary colleges and home economics institute, permitting them to join with a college of arts and science to create one of Ontario's new universities. Guelph's rich heritage came from the land and knowledge applied to practical uses. In 1964 this heritage fused with the traditional disciplines in the humanities, social sciences and physical and biological sciences in a pattern common in Western Canada and the American midwest, but unique in Ontario.

The founding colleges

Macdonald Institute

Johnston tower
Ontario Agricultural College

Ontario Veterinary College

CHAPTER 1

Cowbird, Eagle or Bird of Paradise

The Ontario Agricultural College celebrated its 75th anniversary in June, 1949. Speakers invited for the occasion extolled the achievements of the college and the contributions of its graduates. No one peered into the future or had the temerity to suggest that far-reaching changes might be required.[1]

OAC advertised itself in 1949 as an institution "maintained for the education of Agriculturalists and for the improvement and advancement of Agriculture."[2] Certainly many of OAC's students came directly from farms. The college claimed they received an education similar in many respects to that offered by other colleges or universities, although in an atmosphere that stressed rural life. Students at OAC retained "contact with farm activities, with crops and livestock, with farm equipment and farm-reared folks" in order to foster an "understanding and appreciation of the advantages and joys of farm life as well as of its complex problems."[3] The outdated image portrayed by the college spoke more of the idyllic qualities of a rural life being threatened by advancing industrialization than of the intellectual challenges of the scientific education increasingly required by farmers in the postwar world.

Postwar agriculture in Ontario bore little resemblance to its prewar traditions. Between 1939 and 1975, agricultural production in the province doubled, while the total farm population declined by more than 50 per cent. Land devoted to agriculture also shrank rapidly, as did the number of farms, although the remaining farms grew correspondingly large.[4] The pace of rural change was accelerating, but were agricultural education and research keeping up? This was one of the most serious questions confronting those who were planning ahead for OAC.

Agricultural higher education in Ontario stood apart from the pattern developed in all the western provinces where it was an integral part of the provincial universities. In Ontario, the province deliberately located the agricultural college in a separate community from the provincial university. This isolation permitted the Ontario Agricultural College and its companion institutions, the Ontario Veterinary College and Macdonald Institute, to cater specifically to the needs of agriculture, and it removed each of them from the cross fertilization of scientific research and the exchange of intellectual ideas characteristic of university life.

The Ontario Agricultural College was founded in 1874 in the tradition of the American land grant institutions. These developed rapidly in the United States following the passage of the 1862 Morrill Act, which assigned a portion of the public lands to support agricultural and mechanical education. OAC differed from American institutions in that it was under direct government control. As a result, the education it offered was oriented towards the practical. In its report on the new school of agriculture, the Provincial Farm Commission of 1874 claimed the school tried "to avoid the error of sacrificing the practical to the theoretical."[5] This ascendancy of the practical over the theoretical, which meant a concentration on increasing the efficiency of agricultural production, appealed to farmers and the politicians who were dependent on their votes. It remained the guiding ethos of the college until well into the 20th century. Students attending OAC received an apprenticeship training in farming rather than an education stressing applied theoretical and scientific knowledge. The focus was on animal husbandry, not animal science.

In 1880, the School of Agriculture was re-named the Ontario Agricultural College and affiliated with the University of Toronto. From 1887, OAC students could receive a three-year Bachelor's degree from the University of Toronto. The practical emphasis of the program remained. The college did not follow the lead of the American land grant colleges that developed into state universities and expanded their courses of study into the traditional humanities and the emerging science and social science disciplines. At the college's 25th anniversary, President James Mills stressed his determination to maintain an agricultural curriculum unadulterated by association with any university disciplines, and to keep it practical with an emphasis on manual labour. As it entered the 20th century, OAC firmly rejected the state university example and what it represented. Even the teaching of English had to be defended in 1902 against those who accused the college of concentrating too much on non-agricultural courses.

James Mills was active in working to expand the college's role in educating rural women. He lent his support to Adelaide Hoodless who had pioneered the teaching of home economics in Ontario, and supported the establishment of Macdonald Institute, opened in 1903 to train female teachers for rural schools and to give rural women practical education in domestic science.[6]

After World War I, several developments pointed to a greater emphasis on scientific research and theoretical knowledge. The move of the Ontario Veterinary College to Guelph from Toronto in 1922 firmly tied veterinary medicine to agriculture and brought the reputation of OVC to Guelph. Admission standards were raised for OAC, the degree and diploma courses were separated, and Master's degrees in agriculture were begun in 1926, in collaboration with the University of Toronto. For some people these developments were harbingers of further changes, but the Depression and the Second World War interfered. By the end of the war, the status of OAC and its sister institutions still seemed frozen in a 19th century mould.[7]

All three institutions were colleges of the Department of Agriculture with the faculty and staff part of Ontario's civil service. Government control had its benefits: guaranteed funding; the protection of a major government department; public identification of the activities of the colleges; and teaching, research, and extension as functions essential to the well-being of Ontario's rural population. But to some, there were also very definite drawbacks. Was a civil service atmosphere ideal to undertake world class agricultural research? Was government control compatible with the academic freedom cherished by universities? In a rapidly changing world, would agricultural education and research be able to adjust quickly in a complex and old fashioned bureaucracy that was subject to ministerial control and public regulation? Fears about negative answers to each of these questions caused pressure for reform, even if little of this surfaced from within the institutions themselves.

The real impetus for change came from OAC alumni. All wanted to see the reputation of their alma mater grow. Some were also openly critical of the college. John Kenneth Galbraith, the college's most famous alumnus, publicly savaged the academic reputation of OAC in several magazine articles in 1948.

Galbraith rightly accused the faculty of being "inbred and inert" and blamed the decline "on the relation of the college to the Provincial Department of Agriculture." He caustically wrote that "real scholarship has never flourished in a civil service atmosphere where, as at OAC, men sign in in the morning and dutifully record their hour of departure at night." The economist could not imagine an atmosphere of complete academic freedom where a scientist might have to

consider "the effect of his work on the political fortunes of a superior."
Galbraith also criticized the college's research record, while stressing the fundamental importance of research in the modern world.

> Good research work is the mainspring of the change and
> development which it is the prime task of the college to in-
> itiate. It is also what brings together and maintains the
> community of scientists which, in the last analysis, is what
> a college is.[8]

Galbraith's pen had exposed the weaknesses of his alma mater.
He certainly succeeded in annoying the college's faculty and his fellow alumni, some of whom were working quietly behind the scenes
to press for structural reform. The faculty may not have been as inert
as Galbraith's rhetoric implied, but they were inbred. A report on the
college prepared in 1947 for the minister of agriculture by Dean A.C.
Lewis of the Ontario College of Education found that most of the staff
were graduates of OAC with "little, if any post-graduate training."[9]
    Central to any reform was the relationship between OAC, its
sister institutions at Guelph, and the provincial Department of
Agriculture. The OAC alumni wanted changes in this relationship
from at least the early 1930s. They believed their college should be
run by an independent Board of Governors rather than being under
the minister of agriculture's direct control. All their proposals called
for alumni representatives on the board. In their minds, the college's
independence from government was synonymous with greater
alumni control over its operations.
    Colonel Thomas Kennedy, the longtime Conservative minister
of agriculture, ostensibly sympathized with alumni concerns. He held
the agriculture portfolio in the Ferguson and Henry governments
from 1930-34 and returned to it during the Drew government from
1943-1948. After his own brief period as premier, he continued to
serve as agriculture minister under Leslie Frost until 1953. Shortly
after the Drew government took office, Kennedy had his deputy minister, W.R. Reek, announce the creation of a special committee of inquiry into the future management of OAC on the occasion of the
alumni meeting at the college in June, 1944. The inquiry was chaired
by Reek himself and included the OAC president, George Christie.[10]
    The alumni took advantage of the inquiry to present another
brief advocating an independent board of governors, using as one argument the need to improve research activities at the college. Their
proposal met a favourable reception from the committee and apparently from the minister. Press speculation in advance of the
committee's report predicted that OAC would soon receive full
university status, possibly as the University of Ontario. Kennedy was

reported as being in agreement with the need to remove the college from the political control of the ministry.

The Committee of Inquiry filed its report with the minister early in February, 1945.[11] The main recommendation was a bold step: amalgamation of the three colleges into one institution. Flushed with patriotism, the committee wanted to create either the Royal Ontario College or the Royal Ontario University at Guelph with a Board of Governors, a president and deans of agriculture, veterinary science and home economics. Each college or faculty was to be a separate entity; the deans were to be autonomous and subject only to the powers of co-ordination vested in the president and the board. The report envisaged degree-granting powers for the college, but rather ambiguously suggested the degrees would continue to be granted through the University of Toronto. The independence and viability of such an institution were open to serious question.

Reek, as chairman of the Committee of Inquiry, left a summary of the advantages of operating the colleges under an independent board of governors.[12] A board would mean greater continuity of policy making than was possible under cabinet ministers who changed regularly. It would also give people engaged in agriculture more responsibility for the administration of the colleges. Reek looked forward to greater co-operation between OAC and OVC, which until then, in his view, had operated as two distinct units with very limited co-operation. He also foresaw the possibility of significant private financial support that would reduce the colleges' complete dependence on government funding. Greater co-operation combined with more private revenue would, in Reek's view, lead to significant benefits for Ontario's agricultural industry. Neither Reek nor the other members of his committee identified any possible negative effects.

Although Thomas Kennedy supported these initiatives, he was ill when the report was completed. Reek sent it instead to the acting minister, W.G. Thompson, and requested the attorney general's office to draft legislation to create the new Royal Ontario College. In the 1945 throne speech presented to the Legislature on February 15, the Ontario government included a reference to plans providing for the co-ordinated administration of OAC, OVC and Macdonald Institute. Further support for the creation of a board of governors that would take over administration of the colleges from the government came in an Agricultural Commission of Inquiry, tabled in the Legislature a month later.[13] Everything seemed ready for federation. Then, suddenly the idea was dropped without any public explanation. The bill to implement the changes had not been introduced when the government dissolved the Legislature for a late spring election.

During the election, the question receded as a political issue and when the election was over, it was forgotten at Queen's Park.

The draft bill to create the Royal Ontario College still exists in the ministry of agriculture archives, a ghostly reminder of an institution that never became reality.[14] Even the carefully prepared report of the OAC Committee of Inquiry was quietly shelved and remained hidden in the obscurity of the ministry records. Who scuttled the plan? Years later in the Ontario Legislature, former premier, Harry Nixon, alleged that George McCullagh, the influential publisher of *The Globe and Mail* and a member of the board of governors of the University of Toronto, had "queered the whole thing ... He was not going to let Toronto lose any prestige or status by having this college removed from the university."[15] George Drew's government was not about to incur the wrath of the University of Toronto and the powerful elite on its Board of Governors even to establish a royal college in Drew's birthplace. The Royal Ontario College vanished with scarcely a ripple and never re-surfaced.

Government inaction only deepened the frustration of OAC alumni. Their next real opportunity to influence government to change occurred in an unexpected forum in 1949, the year OAC was celebrating its seventy-fifth anniversary. The select committee of the Ontario Legislature examining conservation throughout the province that year invited public submissions, giving the alumni another opportunity to make their views known, this time to Ontario legislators.

The brief, which the executive of the OAC Alumni Association presented to the select committee in November, 1949, eloquently and forcefully championed the importance of agriculture in Canada's rapidly evolving industrial society. It stressed, not surprisingly, the crucial part played by the Ontario Agricultural College in agricultural education. The authors underlined, however, their conviction that OAC itself had to be transformed, an action that could only be accomplished by government. The college "must take the lead in formulating agricultural educational policy to suit the needs of a highly industrialized age ... no longer can the Ontario Agricultural College be considered purely as a training ground for young farmers."[16]

The alumni still wanted to establish the college as a distinct body with a Senate and an independent Board of Governors responsible only to the Ontario cabinet. By making the college a unique provincial university — the brief even suggested naming it the University of Ontario — its mandate would be wide-ranging and once again the Ontario Agricultural College would be "the envy and attraction of thinking people throughout the world." It could also be "a great centre where research, development and propagation of conservation ideas and techniques may be found."[17]

The Alumni Association saw a state agricultural university as a means of recapturing lost prestige, while providing the province with vigorous leadership in agricultural research. The authors wrote:

> A university must be a proving ground, the shooting range of new ideas. There must be an obvious degree of freedom from outside interference and obligation to create the desired atmosphere so essential to the development of new ideas and new conceptions. The institution at Guelph must be set up so that it cannot become a tool of any farm group, labour group or financial group. It must represent the interests of all and must be represented by all interests.[18]

It was in some ways a radical vision and ahead of its time for Ontario. The alumni were convinced that "an expanded, revitalized and independent" Ontario Agricultural College with "prestige and financial resources equal to a great university" would give the agricultural and scientific leadership the province and the country required. It would not happen as long as the college remained shackled by its dependency on the Department of Agriculture. The association's vice-president, Fred W. Presant, made this plain in testimony before the select committee:

> The OAC is still the only institution of its kind in North America whereby the minister of agriculture exerts the controlling factor in its administration — which leaves an unstable policy and [makes it] subject to the personalities of one man.[19]

The same mixture of hope for the prospects of an independent OAC and frustration with the control exercised by the Department of Agriculture appeared in the Ontario Federation of Agriculture's brief to the select committee. "We do not know of any other College that is directly responsible to a Cabinet Minister and no independent Board."[20] The federation wanted an independent board of governors and financing for OAC on the basis of "a straight gift from the government with no strings attached." Its brief did not advocate immediate university status, but it was a likely possibility in the long term. It believed the new board of governors should be empowered to resolve issues such as the college's affiliation with the University of Toronto and the appointment of a senate.

These two briefs set an agenda for change for the Ontario Agricultural College, an agenda that would take fifteen years to complete. Change for OAC was bound to affect OVC and Macdonald Institute. OAC itself also prepared a brief for the select committee, but the college document stuck strictly to conservation issues and scrupulously avoided any comment on the college structure.

The select committee presented its report in 1950. It chose to include a recommendation on the three Guelph institutions, even though it deftly deflected the university question, "leaving that to be decided at a future date in the light of future experience."[21] The committee believed the idea of a university at Guelph was premature, but it did recommend the federation of the three Guelph colleges into one institution with a president and three deans. Under a federation, the committee believed the three colleges would "assume greater stature," a goal apparently everyone agreed was desirable.

Federation, too, was still an idea ahead of its time, but its inclusion in a select committee report, favourably received in the province, was later taken to indicate both official and public acceptance of the consolidation of the Guelph colleges. University status had not been endorsed by the Legislature, but neither had it been rejected. Sadly, what was lost sight of in the report and in the events of the next few years was the Alumni Association's vision of what this new university might be. Nevertheless, the Alumni Association's brief of 1949 marked the real beginning of an administrative process that would culminate in the creation of the University of Guelph fifteen years later.

Nobody better personified the determination and vision of the Alumni Association than its vice-president in 1949, Fred W. Presant. He graduated from the college in 1923, after serving in the First World War, and by 1949 was vice-president of the Toronto Elevators Company. His commitment to his alma mater was evident in his work on the brief. In 1950, he became president of the Alumni Association and was asked to serve on the Advisory Board created that year by the minister of agriculture. Presant soon became chairman and went on to chair a subsequent board in the mid-1950s and the Board of Regents of the Federated Colleges from 1962-64. In 1964 he was named to the first Board of Governors of the university. As chairman of the various boards advising the minister during these years, Presant worked tirelessly in a voluntary role to implement the alumni vision of what OAC might become. His contributions were important in the transformations that culminated in university status.

In 1950, John Kenneth Galbraith fired another broadside at his alma mater. Speaking before the annual convention of the Canadian Federation of Agriculture at Niagara Falls on February 1, Galbraith said: "It is one of the tragedies of agriculture that the Ontario Agricultural College has been allowed to go into decay." The *Toronto Daily Star* gave headline treatment to Galbraith's blast[22] and the *Farmer's Advocate* devoted a large part of one issue to an examination of his charges. Although the *Farmer's Advocate* did not support Galbraith's indictment, it did favour a more intensified research role for the college. For this reason, the *Advocate* hoped "the brakes" on OAC would soon be released in order to permit it to undertake more intellectual and scientific research.[23] The "brakes," of course, were the tight controls exercised by the government.

The students at Guelph were ahead of the politicians. In 1950 they founded a student paper, *The Ontarion*, to represent student views in all three Guelph institutions. They excavated the basement of Massey Hall for a student union, making their own moves toward a unified Guelph campus, even if the institutions themselves were still separate.

The select committee report planted the seed of institutional change, but it was up to the institutions themselves to cultivate it under the direct and absolute control of the minister of agriculture. Both OAC and OVC were legislative creations of the Ontario government and no real institutional change could occur without legislative amendments. They were not free to initiate change and in the early 1950s it was not at all clear that anyone within the colleges really wanted basic alterations in their status.

Institutional change came so slowly as to be almost imperceptible, and it is only in retrospect that one can discern a pattern of evolution leading to the creation of an independent university. The Leslie Frost government, which took office in Ontario in 1949, considered the status of the Guelph colleges. But Frost was always cautious about making changes that affected rural Ontario, and neither Frost nor his first minister of agriculture, Colonel Kennedy, was prepared to contemplate university status or federation. Not even the idea of an independent board of governors held any appeal. Some action, however, was necessary to meet the demands of the OAC alumni and the Ontario Federation of Agriculture.

On August 25, 1950, the minister of agriculture announced the creation of an OAC Advisory Board to be composed of the following members: at least three alumni, the deputy minister of agriculture, the chief director of the Ontario Department of Education, the director of research for the Ontario Department of Agriculture and the president of OAC. The department gave up none of its authority over the college since the board's role was to advise the minister. The board contained a high-powered group of individuals and, most importantly, it gave key members of the alumni an important vehicle for making their views known. In reality it became an embryonic board of governors, even if it lacked the authority to make decisions. The press release announcing formation of the board made no mention whatever of any criticism of the college or desires for change in its status. The board's creation occurred, according to the Department of Agriculture, because of the great increase in the college's activities. Tucked away in the press release was an important recognition by the Department of Agriculture that "research is the lifeblood of all teaching and extension."[24] Although Galbraith's name was not mentioned, this was a discreet public acknowledgement that his criticisms had been heard within the government as well as within his alma mater. Research would assume a much more prominent place in the work of the college from then on.

Once the Advisory Board became a reality, the alumni stopped pursuing university status. Fred Presant remembers how the alumni perceived the original Advisory Board. "We just wanted that body in there who could come down and on behalf of the administration, tell the minister whatever had to be told, and it wouldn't reflect on the administrator's head because he couldn't go and talk to them like that. We could. We were an independent body. Well, we had nothing to lose."[25] The board was to be the college's advocate with the Department of Agriculture and its minister, speaking for the president and the faculty.

A central element in the effectiveness of the Advisory Board was the rapport between its members and the president of the Ontario Agricultural College. When alumni of OAC learned in 1950 that the minister of agriculture was about to appoint a new president of the college and heard names of possible candidates, they expressed their concerns directly to Colonel Kennedy. Fred Presant, one of the alumni involved, recalls what happened:

> We heard rumours that emanated from the minister of agriculture's office that there had been two or three people named as possible candidates for this office. None of these people, in the minds of the alumni group who were interested in this matter, was felt to be satisfactory. It was because of this that we asked for and received an opportunity to meet with the minister privately in his own home one Sunday afternoon out in Islington and talk about it.[26]

Following this conversation, Kennedy named Presant along with two other members of the alumni executive, Acting President Reek, and Deputy Minister Cliff Graham as a committee to go to Guelph and select the best candidate. They unanimously recommended the name of Dr. John D. MacLachlan. Kennedy announced MacLachlan's appointment in June and he became president of the college on September 1, 1950.

As the alumni's choice, Dr. MacLachlan clearly was able to work effectively and closely with the Advisory Board. MacLachlan, who had a Ph.D. in plant pathology from Harvard, was one of OAC's most distinguished scholars. He came to the presidency with eleven years of teaching and administrative experience at the college. He was to serve in succession as president of OAC, the Federated Colleges, and the University of Guelph during a seventeen-year period of profound transformation.

Macdonald Institute and OVC also experienced continuity in leadership during the transition period of the 1950s. MacLachlan's long tenure as president of OAC was matched by those of Trevor Lloyd Jones and Margaret McCready. After ten years service as director of Household Science at Macdonald College of McGill University, Margaret McCready came to Guelph in 1949 as principal of Macdonald Institute, a position she retained until the campus reorganization of the 1960s when she became dean of Macdonald College. Trevor Lloyd Jones served a two-year stint as acting principal of the Ontario Veterinary College from 1950-52, during the illness of Principal McNabb. On McNabb's death in 1952, Jones was confirmed as principal and held this position for ten years until he became dean of the Ontario Veterinary College.

Even though all three colleges were equally subordinate to the Department of Agriculture and its minister, they were not perceived as equal from the viewpoint of Queen's Park. Discussions on the status of the colleges focused particularly on OAC, which in the eyes of the politicians and civil servants, had a special importance. Macdonald Institute and its principal had a difficult time making their voices heard in Toronto and Margaret McCready was given very little opportunity to influence the direction of the change the colleges were about to experience.

The Ontario Veterinary College shared some of the problems faced by OAC. Trevor Lloyd Jones recalling how inbred the veterinary college was, said: "We were incestuous." One of his main priorities was to improve faculty qualifications and hire new faculty from a mixture of places instead of relying solely on OVC graduates. He arranged a program of leaves for faculty who wanted to raise their qualifications and he hired "definitively trained people" from the United States, Australia and Britain as well as Canada. "We had a regular United Nations of faculty."[27]

Jones thought that neither OAC nor OVC was conducting very much scientific research prior to the 1950s. He remembers OAC having the best demonstration animals of any agricultural college he knew, but its reputation largely rested on this and the agricultural training and extension services it provided. The situation was similar in the veterinary college. Scientific research had to overcome considerable obstacles. When one of the ablest faculty members at OVC,

Dr. Frank Schofield, was hard pressed to find money to buy calves to carry on his work, he persuaded the sympathetic deputy minister of agriculture to add $2,000 to the college budget. But when Schofield found the money was not available, the principal of the day said: "Where do you think I got the money to repair the college toilets?"[28]

The new governing structure of the Ontario Agricultural College helped to change the atmosphere of the campus. The OAC Advisory Board, chaired by Fred Presant, became a convenient forum to discuss problems and policies brought to its attention by Dr. MacLachlan. Through these discussions, the college benefited from the advice given by alumni and government administrators. It soon became much more than a passive vehicle to ratify the president's policies. Three years later, in 1953, a report prepared for the minister itemized nineteen areas in which recommendations had been made. All seventeen departments of OAC had been appraised, the college administration had been examined in detail, the facilities, curriculum and scholarships had all been studied and new buildings had been planned. One of the first tasks had been a thorough analysis of the academic salary schedule and the preparation of a new schedule to raise salaries. In its accompanying justification, the board pointed to the importance of the faculty:

> ... If the Ontario Agricultural College is to become one of the best on the continent, it must draw to its staff, and hold, some of the best men available in each of the various fields of academic and research activities. A college or university is "great" not because of its physical facilities alone, but because of the calibre of the members of its faculty.[29]

The Advisory Board articulated the aspirations of alumni to see their institution become recognized as one of the leading agricultural colleges in North America. The board requested legislative recognition at the end of December, 1951, justifying this as a further step in the OAC quest to achieve "its rightful position of leadership among the continent's leading institutions for agricultural education and research."[30] If this goal was to be achieved, future planning was vital.

One of the most vigorous advocates of systematic planning for the future was another alumni board member. Dr. Reginald Stratford, who had been Imperial Oil's first research chemist and achieved national stature, served as director of research and subsequently as a scientific adviser to Imperial Oil. He was a member of the OAC Advisory Board from its beginning until his death in 1959. In 1954 he received the Society of Chemical Industry's gold medal for outstanding scientific and industrial achievement. His far-sighted ideas on research and agricultural education helped to lay the groundwork for the future university. As a member of the Ontario Research Commission in 1948, Stratford vigorously defended OAC against Galbraith's attacks, while agreeing with Galbraith's conclusion "that it is better for a seat of learning to be separated from a department of government; many of the alumni of the college will agree with this."[31]

Although agreement was general that OAC should strive to become a continental leader in agricultural education, the methods of achieving this lofty ideal were less easy to identify. All the members of the Advisory Board were asked in June, 1953 for their views on future terms of reference for the board. Stratford's reply focused on the key issue. Within a year, the board should prepare specific recommendations on how OAC should be organized and operated and "whether or not it should have full university status."[32] Stratford added:

> In my opinion the Ontario Agricultural College at Guelph can never regain and maintain its position as one of the great agricultural institutions on this continent unless it is prepared for a thorough housecleaning from attic to cellar, and until there is proper recognition [of the role] such an institution devoted to Agricultural science can and should play in the province.[33]

The issue of whether or not to seek university status continued to nag the OAC Advisory Board members. It was the central question they had to resolve in planning for the future. Both Dr. MacLachlan and Reginald Stratford visited Europe in the early 1950s to examine agricultural education. MacLachlan toured England, Denmark, Scotland and Holland in the summer of 1952, but as he admitted himself, he was more interested at the time in the European outlook on agriculture than on examining university status.

Stratford, on the other hand, in a visit the following year, probed European methods of agricultural education in a search for examples to guide those planning the future of OAC. He visited agricultural schools and universities in Denmark, Holland and Sweden, as well as Britain. Following his return, he wrote a paper entitled "OAC: Present Status and Proposals for the Future." His paper looked at the question of whether OAC should try to be an agricultural technical college or aim at becoming an agricultural university. Europe offered precedents for both. After reviewing each alternative, Stratford candidly told the board "he was uncertain in his own mind which objective best suited the college, that of aspiring to be merely a practical agricultural college, or that of university status."[34]

At least one other board member favoured the idea of OAC becoming a technical college and maintaining government ties. Deputy Minister of Agriculture C. O. Graham, who sat on the board, observed that a university would not appeal to younger men who wanted to return to the farm or become extension specialists. The discussion on Stratford's paper was inconclusive. There certainly was no groundswell of support for launching a university, but the issue was one that would not disappear.

There were very few signs of student interest in university status during the early 1950s. In 1952, however, the student newspaper ran a spoof issue under the headline "The University of Ontario." An editorial advocated a University of Ontario to replace the "three bodied headless creature which [was] the student body of the campus." Not all readers were amused. Two letters in the next issue criticized the paper. One called for a concentration on the expression of "more mature and rational ideas" and the other recommended concentrating on the present and not on a "too far removed future."[35]

The university issue arose again in the spring of 1953 when the Advisory Board created three sub-committees to report on research, the federation of the three colleges, and the OAC teaching program. This was done in response to a motion by Reginald Stratford to prepare "a clear-cut, comprehensive report on the desirable future development of the college" for the minister of agriculture.[36] Fred Presant, chairman of the Advisory Board, put himself on the sub-committee examining the federation of the three colleges. His report was based on the premise that federation was a desirable goal.[37] He began by recapping the history of the idea in the OAC alumni brief of 1949 and the response of the Select Committee on Conservation. Because of the "peculiar situation" of the ownership of all the physical plant by the government and the complete reliance on and accountability to the government, Presant saw no practical way of changing the status of OAC for the moment. The report did, however, recommend federation to improve the efficiency of the colleges' operations, and the creation of a board of governors, although there was no desire to change the degree-granting power exercised by the University of Toronto. With federation of the three institutions, "general policy making, future planning and development, and integrated problems of administration could be developed through to a central head."[38]

This report and its two companion pieces on research and teaching were formally adopted at the September meeting of the Advisory Board, attended by Fletcher Thomas, the minister of agriculture. Thomas was familiar with Guelph and with the ideas of the OAC alumni. Fred Presant told the board that the possibility of university status was a long-term prospect, but that before it could become reality, a lot more detailed planning was necessary. He argued much more strongly for federation and an independent board of governors. Thomas's reply was that university status could not be considered "just now." He was willing to contemplate the principle of federation, but he believed a new board was necessary to work out the mechanics. This new board would represent each of the institutions, study their joint problems and make recommendations to the minister. There was still no thought whatsoever of the ministry giving up any iota of political control.

Members of the Advisory Board backed federation as a step in the right direction. None of them as individuals, let alone the board itself as a collective entity, challenged the minister by pushing for more radical or faster change. The evolutionary process would continue even if few observers inside or outside the colleges could perceive it happening. One new note had been struck, however, by Reginald Stratford in the discussions on federation. He raised the need for a university college or department of humanities that would embrace the arts, languages and social sciences and serve the three existing colleges.

The Department of Agriculture's suggestion of a new governing body took form the following year in an awkwardly named group entitled the Pro Tem Advisory Committee on Co-ordination. It had no real power except to advise the minister, but its role was to explore ways to bring the three Guelph colleges closer together. By 1956 it had become a permanent structure, as cumbersome and complex as its title suggested — the Advisory Board for Conjoint Administration. The department also created advisory committees for OVC and Macdonald Institute to go along with the one for OAC, which remained in place. This structure of advisory boards and committees continued unchanged for the next six years. In spite of an unwieldy name, the lack of any authority and the problem of overlapping interests, the advisory board functioned as effectively as it could and played a valuable role in helping President MacLachlan develop proposals for a new institution at Guelph.

MacLachlan had begun to visualize the shape of a new campus even before the Department of Agriculture re-structured the advisory boards. He realized that new buildings would be needed, and early in 1955 he presented the OAC Advisory Board with a proposal for a unified campus, the first attempt to identify the physical or concrete components of the future university.[39] MacLachlan identified five key faculty units for the new campus. These included the three existing colleges — agriculture, veterinary science and household sciences —

a faculty of extension services, and a humanities faculty that would be "neutral on the campus," integrating their services with the three older faculties.

Neither President MacLachlan's very practical idea of what a new campus would contain, nor the complex structure of committees designed to ensure co-operation among the three Guelph colleges, answered the fundamental question of the future objectives of the institutions, especially OAC. The one person on the Advisory Board who kept asking this question throughout the 1950s, without answering it clearly, was Reginald Stratford. He wrote a memorandum for the board in 1956, still arguing the need to "define more clearly the objective of the OAC."

> Should it have university status for the training of agricultural scientists with facilities to grant advanced degrees? Should it be a practical college for the training of scientific farmers or should it continue to carry on the many functions that it is burdened with at the present time, such as teaching degree courses and associated students, the operation of large experimental units and advisory services?[40]

The Advisory Board did not confront Stratford's issues directly, but it soon found itself carried along by outside events and thrust into planning for a university without being certain yet of the objective.

In 1955, Edward Sheffield, then employed by the Dominion Bureau of Statistics, presented a paper to the National Conference on Canadian Universities, predicting the doubling of university enrolment within a decade. Sheffield sounded a warning that was listened to across Canada, and governments, both provincial and federal, suddenly woke up to the urgent need for new facilities to meet the flood of students who would want to attend university in the next ten to twenty years.[41] The Ontario government did its own projections and also forecast a doubling of university enrolment over the next decade. These projections then formed the basis of the Ontario submission to the Gordon Royal Commission on Canada's Economic Prospects that same year. One of those who was enlightened by these statistical projections was University of Toronto President Sidney Smith.[42] He became convinced that the University of Toronto would have to expand, but he knew this move alone would not meet the demand.

It was Sidney Smith, aware of the desperate need for additional facilities to accommodate a new generation of university students, and possibly acting with the knowledge and support of leading officials of the Ontario government, who wrote to President MacLachlan early in 1957, urging him to think in terms of a university. His letter was a gentle prod that MacLachlan took to heart and included in his later submission to the Ontario Government. Smith wrote:

> I do think that it would be wise for you to explore now the possibility of combining Ontario Agricultural College, Ontario Veterinary College and Macdonald Institute in one institution with degree-granting powers. Such an egg would take some time to hatch, whatever be the hatcher — cowbird, eagle or Bird of Paradise. If I were at Queen's Park and I were looking over the university scene in Ontario, I would be bound, I am sure, to come to the conclusion that it would be less expensive to develop your institutions into an independent university than it would be to start a new university or universities.[43]

Smith's letter contained the same utilitarian justification that would be heard time and again in the next seven years. Guelph already had many university facilities; consequently, it would be cheaper to build a university there than start from scratch anywhere else in the province. Cost was a primary consideration and the argument was certainly valid; indeed, if anything, it became stronger during the early 1960s when the pressure on government intensified. For harried politicians and their advisers, the utilitarian argument carried the risk of being the only argument that would convince them to build a university at Guelph.

J. D. MacLachlan recalled that he first thought seriously of the possibility of a university for Guelph after being encouraged by President Sidney Smith of Toronto. At a Faculty Club luncheon held at the University of Toronto early in 1957, President Smith leaned across the table and suddenly asked, "Mac, when are you going to design a university at Guelph?" MacLachlan replied, "perhaps in the early sixties when pressure for university space becomes more acute." Smith's response was prophetic: "that will be too late for me to help you, Mac."[44] Smith, of course, did not know that he would not live past 1959, but his urgency affected MacLachlan who began for the first time to think in terms of the transformation of the Guelph campus into a university. The enthusiastic support of Sidney Smith, whom he liked and admired, was an important ingredient in MacLachlan's own conversion.

Sidney Smith's letter was the forerunner of more official interest. The subject of OAC came up again in the legislature in 1957. A Liberal opposition member criticized the college during the debate on the Speech from the Throne and suggested the appointment of an "up-to-date" board of governors rather than the continuation of what he labelled as a political machine.[45] The newly appointed minister of agriculture, William Goodfellow, a Codrington farmer and OAC alumnus, responded to this attack when he brought in the estimates for the Department of Agriculture. He claimed that the creation of a board of governors had been given a preliminary examination and hinted that he personally favoured the idea. He then tossed out a more tantalizing prospect. If a board was appointed, "it would naturally follow" that the three institutions "would in the fullness of time" become a university. He quickly reassured the Legislature that this would in no way be to the detriment of agriculture. Even as a university, the colleges "must always retain their agricultural influence and the importance of agriculture."[46]

The opposition welcomed the announcement as freeing OAC in particular from the evils of political interference. Typical was the pronouncement by the former Liberal premier of the province, Harry Nixon:

> I think the time is long overdue when we should have this under a board of governors and recognize it as the university of agriculture, so that the professors and others there are not considered by anybody as civil servants any more than those at the University of Toronto are so considered.[47]

Many members of the colleges applauded the prospect of being removed from direct political control, although there was more than a little irony in the strong Liberal support. College faculty had been vulnerable not only to political pressure exercised in subtle ways through the Department of Agriculture, but also to political attacks from Opposition members in the Legislature eager to score political points on the government at the expense of OAC. In 1956, for example, the Liberal Leader of the Opposition, Farquhar Oliver, used the debate on the Department of Agriculture estimates to criticize a speech given by the head of the Agricultural Economics Department, Professor D.R. Campbell. Premier Frost stepped in to defend Campbell, equating him with a university professor:

> There is never an attempt made to regiment university professors. They are very independent, and they reserve the right to say what they want to say, when and how they want to say it.[48]

Campbell had organized a high profile workshop for Ontario farm leaders. He spoke on the topic, "Are there too many farmers in Ontario" and concluded that there were. As he recalls, "that caused a great stir because it was the first time that anybody publicly had made those comments. Many farm leaders said 'well, I don't agree with you but you have the right to express your own views!' One farmer that I know, a very nice friend, said, 'I don't know whether we've got too many farmers, but I think we've got too many farm economists.' "[49]

The university question now moved from the Legislature to Guelph. Following his announcement in the Legislature, Goodfellow visited Guelph and met with the Advisory Board to bring it up to date on the government's thinking. Presant, the chairman of the board, told Goodfellow that "considerable discussion, speculation, and stimulated interest had been evidenced, however, in the possibilities of university status."[50] Goodfellow, in turn, requested the board to carry out a confidential assessment of the possibility of transforming the Guelph colleges into a university.

His request for confidentiality, which the members of the advisory boards and committees honoured, constrained everyone, including the college heads, in their actions. They did not feel free to initiate a public campaign, nor did they arrange for open discussion of the implications of university status within the colleges. What they could and did do was to begin planning as civil servants, sending their advice through to the minister for the government to make the final decisions. Goodfellow's request for confidentiality had one overriding purpose: to leave the government free to accept or reject a plan for university status at Guelph. What neither he nor the administrators or board members at Guelph foresaw was the danger of springing a university plan for OAC upon the agricultural public of Ontario without any advance preparation. Confidentiality also prevented the mobilization of local community support, so important an element in other Ontario centres where new universities were being launched.

Goodfellow's announcement about the possible future of the Guelph colleges did not go unnoticed in the rest of the province. A farm editorial in *The Simcoe Reformer* late in April caught the ambiguity that had hung over OAC, its faculty and alumni since the issue first surfaced after the war.

> Some move, such as the one now under consideration, has been overdue for years. This is the opinion of some, while others think the Ontario Agricultural College should be left as it is.[51]

The *Reformer* thought it was time "the apron string arrangement" with the Ontario Department of Agriculture came to an end, and welcomed the prospect of a university "if the idea is allowed to develop naturally and normally." But if OAC was to be made a university, the paper felt the Department of Agriculture could not continue to run it:

A university is a college of scholars, not civil servants. In essence the work of a government department is to administer the law. Education flourishes in an atmosphere quite different; one of free inquiry, primarily concerned with the development of the human mind. If a new university does develop on the Guelph site, it is hoped that the Ontario Agricultural College will not be denied the opportunity to participate directly in its life and collective responsibilities.[52]

In the 1940s, OAC alumni had a clear vision of what their college should be — a state agricultural university providing leadership in agricultural teaching and research. Once key members of the alumni were given a say in the direction of the college through membership on the Advisory Board, their commitment to university status dissipated. Between 1950 and 1956, the Advisory Board did not commit itself to the goal of becoming a university. The closest it came was to reiterate support for the federation of the three colleges in 1954. The change in 1957 came from outside forces — the suggestion of the president of the University of Toronto, the request of the minister of agriculture to examine the possibility, and the knowledge of all associated with the three colleges that they could not escape the implications of the looming enrolment crisis of Canadian universities. The change, however, was real. Beginning in 1957, officials and board members began to think and plan for a university at Guelph.

CHAPTER 2

Planning a State University

When the OAC Advisory Committee met in Guelph for one of its quarterly meetings in September, 1957, the most important item on its agenda was the request of the minister of agriculture for a discreet assessment of university status for the three Guelph colleges. Discretion meant confidentiality. The preparation of plans for a state university during the next two years was carried out by the heads of the institutions acting with their advisory committees and government officials. Faculty members knew little about the proposals and without public discussion the community at large was left in total ignorance. However, President MacLachlan and committee members had a pretty clear idea of the type of university they wanted to create.

Three themes surfaced in the September, 1957 discussions. Each would recur throughout the next seven years. First, was the primacy of agriculture. The tradition and purpose of OAC and its sister institutions were closely bound up with agriculture. Whatever shape a university assumed, agriculture had to play a prominent role. Closely linked to agriculture was the idea of a special connection to rural Ontario. The major universities of the province — Toronto, Queen's and Western — and the newly developing institutions — McMaster, Carleton, Ottawa and Waterloo — were all associated with urban areas and catered to a primarily urban student body. Members of the Advisory Committee believed the Guelph institutions, with their strengths and tradition, could occupy a unique niche among Ontario universities by identifying with rural Ontario. A slowly developing vision of another provincial university was resurfacing, a state university for agriculture serving the whole province alongside the University of Toronto.

These were the tentative aspirations voiced by the Advisory Committee in the first serious discussions of university status. The members unanimously agreed on the need for preliminary planning, if for no other reason than to assess the potential impact of the predicted expansion of university enrolment on the Guelph colleges over the next decade. President MacLachlan was asked to begin the planning process and to identify what a university at Guelph might look like.[1]

Student views on the possibility of university status were not solicited, but in a debate held in 1957 on the resolution "that the three colleges should become faculties of a Guelph University," the opposition won. The arguments in favour were familiar ones — the need for more universities, the location and size of the Guelph campus, and the benefits from additional faculties and degree-granting privileges. The opposing argument, which carried the day, focused on the reputation and prestige of the existing colleges and the need for "better agriculture rather than more universities" in south central Ontario.[2] Student pressure was not the key force pushing the administration towards university status.

By December, 1957, however, the OAC Advisory Committee had committed itself to press for a university. It passed a motion unanimously recommending university status as "the most desirable objective" of the Guelph colleges.[3] A research committee consisting of the heads of the institutions and the chairmen of the advisory committees was struck to prepare plans. The committee worked over the winter and President MacLachlan reported in March, 1958 on the progress it had made. He was able to give the members of the OAC Advisory Committee a much fuller picture of the type of university he believed would suit the Guelph campus. MacLachlan remained committed to the concept of a non-sectarian state university endowed by government appropriation and dependent on the provincial Department of Public Works for its capital facilities. This, of course, was the way the Ontario Agricultural College and its sister institutions had always operated. MacLachlan's state university in some respects simply represented a continuation of the *status quo*. There was certainly greater security and less possibility for disruption within the government fold, but would the provincial government welcome a proposal for a university that operated in a completely different fashion from all the other universities in the province? The question was never openly discussed in meetings between Guelph officials and government administrators, but it was to prove a major obstacle to the achievement of university status.

What MacLachlan termed a state university was not only a continuation of the *status quo*; the idea took on additional force because it was seen by its Guelph advocates as the best way to protect the interests of agriculture in an increasingly industrial Ontario. This defensiveness about agriculture's position emerged even in the discussions at the OAC Advisory Committee. The chairman, Fred Presant, articulated the anxiety of both alumni and many others in the agricultural community when he said "the OAC could not afford to become submerged in the tide of incoming arts students."[4] Presant stressed the importance of making the arts and science faculty complementary to the agricultural programs rather than the other way around. What he said represented more than a natural concern about aggressive newcomers dislodging the long-standing tenant. As long as the colleges had existed on their own, the primacy of agriculture went unquestioned. Now that they were thinking about a transformation into a university, some OAC administrators and alumni on the Advisory Committee feared that the pressure of numbers of arts and science students, combined with the needs of new faculties, might push agriculture into the background. They were determined to prevent this from occurring. If one thing united them, it was the importance of maintaining the pre-eminence of agriculture and the traditional focus on rural Ontario.

Fred Presant went further than his fellow committee members. He expressed optimism that a state agricultural university would kindle the rebirth of agriculture in the province in years ahead and reverse the population movement from rural to urban centres by helping to improve rural economic and social conditions. In some ways, Presant and those who shared his views hoped to recreate what they saw as a better world, one where rural values dominated and agriculture was the primary industry. Turning the clock back was impossible, however, for that world had vanished. These early discussions did not address the questions of how best to adapt agricultural teaching and research to the new industrial Ontario and how to change agricultural education so that it might thrive in a university environment. The tone of defensiveness and the sense that agriculture required special protection did not abate as planning for the university progressed. These fears tempered the excitement that planning a new university would normally have engendered. University status carried increased prestige, but the ambivalence about the place of agriculture in the university, which in turn reflected an unease about the place of agriculture in Ontario society, accounted in part for the cautious approach in designing the university.

MacLachlan's plan for the university envisaged the three existing colleges, which would retain their identities, and three new faculties. The Arts and Science Faculty would include some subjects already taught at OAC and some new ones. There would also be a

Faculty of Engineering and a university-wide Faculty of Graduate Studies. All would function within a unified administration under the governance of a senate for academic affairs and a board of governors for all other matters. The board, however, was to be named by the government and would be responsible to the minister of agriculture. The university would possess its own degree-granting powers and affiliation with the University of Toronto would end.

President MacLachlan did not want to build a large university. To retain the rural traditions exemplified by OAC, he thought a university of 3,000 students would be optimal, especially since a very high proportion of these would be in residence. Guelph did not possess a large enough housing stock to cope with a huge influx of university students for eight months of the year. MacLachlan also wanted the new buildings, especially the academic ones, to fit within the already well established architectural pattern of the campus. He foresaw a Humanities Building of limestone to strengthen the limestone horseshoe of the main campus. His goal was a small residential university located in a beautiful semi-rural setting, and populated with high quality students.

When the Advisory Board overseeing the three institutions endorsed the plan presented by President MacLachlan, the board chairman sent the gist of it to W.A. Goodfellow, the minister of agriculture, in March, 1958.[5] Presant's letter was the first official response to the minister's request a year earlier for an assessment of university status. Presant began by referring to the anticipated pressure for expansion of Ontario's university facilities and the relatively minor costs of transforming Guelph into a university when compared to the cost of building a new institution from scratch. He suggested that in new capital facilities, Guelph would only need a Humanities Building, for which financial support from the Canada Council was available, and additional residence accommodation. The message was clear, and it was an attractive one to a government worried about the immense costs of meeting a rapidly rising demand for university places. Guelph's conversion to a university would be cheap and could be done quickly.

Presant then moved to what was the central issue of university status for him and others connected with the three institutions:

> Throughout the extended histories of the three Colleges, all have been identified not only within this province but beyond, as primarily serving agriculture and rural living. Even an expanded institution of university status could keep attuned to rural needs rather than strictly urban. Any future growth therefore should not be permitted to submerge such a principle.[6]

Presant was preaching to the converted. Goodfellow and officials in his ministry had no intention of allowing university status at Guelph to obscure the central role of agriculture. Presant went on to summarize the key elements of MacLachlan's proposed university:

1. A state university with a particular focus on rural Ontario.

2. A simple and direct university governing structure.

3. The preservation of the identities of the existing three colleges.

4. A new organization for agricultural research, extension and service courses, along with the existing agricultural diploma courses to be worked out.

5. The accountability of Guelph institutions to the government through the minister of agriculture rather than the minister of education.

A month later, Fred Presant met personally with the minister to discuss the ramifications of the proposal. Goodfellow promised to take up the question with his cabinet colleagues. At the same time he asked Presant to have the Advisory Committee submit a report with its recommendations.

Early in May, Goodfellow wrote to Education Minister W. J. Dunlop and Premier Leslie Frost, summarizing what had happened.[7] Dunlop's reply made clear that he had no intention of causing difficulties. He told his cabinet colleague: "The initiative is yours. I could not for a moment suggest doing anything which would upset, or detract from, the success of the present set-up."[8] Premier Frost was more cautious: he wanted to examine the Advisory Committee's report before he was even prepared to discuss the matter.[9]

Presant, helped by President MacLachlan, submitted a nine-page feasibility study to the minister in the middle of June, 1958, outlining the framework on which they proposed to create a University at Guelph. Presant added that "the Board has already considered the matter with sufficient thoroughness to be confident that its proposals are both realistic and feasible."[10]

Before the document was finalized, members of the Advisory Board were canvassed for their suggestions on a possible name for the new university. A number of suggestions were received, but none was formally adopted. Most reflected the desire for a state university stressing agriculture. They included the Rural University of Ontario, the Ontario University of Agriculture and the University of Agricultural Ontario. University of Ontario and Ontario Provincial University were throwbacks to earlier plans for a state university. Also included was University of Guelph, and two attempts to promote a royal flavour — Royal University and Queen Elizabeth University.

But more important than the name at this stage was the organization of the proposed campus.

Each of the three founding colleges would retain its identity and traditional role. The new Faculty of Arts and Sciences would have as its primary objective the provision of educational programs for prospective secondary school teachers. For Advisory Board members this was "in keeping with the objective of projecting the identity of the university to rural Ontario as a whole." Capital needs were specified in a humanities building, a new library and additional residence accommodation. The new residences were linked to the university's rural role. "In keeping with the concept of a rural university for Ontario as a whole, a high proportion of the student body could be expected to come from various parts of the province." The brief foresaw a residence population of 75 per cent male and 25 per cent female, reflecting the proportion of the 1950s, but failing to predict the rapid expansion of female undergraduate enrolment in the next two decades. Eighty per cent of the total student population would be accommodated in residence.

A few small essentially liberal arts universities were developing across Ontario in urban centres, or were on the drawing board. But Guelph's was the only proposal for a state-run university catering specifically to the needs of rural Ontario to emerge in the decade of the largest expansion in postsecondary education Ontario had ever known. Like all other proposals for new universities, this one was dependent on government approval. How did the Conservative government of Leslie Frost respond to the Guelph initiative?

The ministers of agriculture and education, Goodfellow and Dunlop, certainly appeared to favour the conversion of Guelph to a university. Because provincial treasurer James Allan was an OAC graduate, he was also included in meetings. Informal discussion among these cabinet ministers occurred during the summer of 1958. By the end of September, the Cabinet Committee on Universities had met to discuss the proposal with the three ministers and their deputies all in attendance.

Goodfellow declared his support first for the integration of the three existing colleges with a subsequent expansion to a university. He accepted the principle that without an arts faculty it would not be a university. This discussion raised a problem the ministers were unable to overcome: OAC would continue to receive support from provincial funds and an arts faculty responsible to a board of governors would also receive all its funding from provincial grants. There was no desire in the Frost government to have the province directly fund a university in Guelph differently from the rest of the province's universities. A state agricultural university was certainly a possibility, but the colleges required an arts faculty to become a university, and the government refused to contemplate financing it through the Department of Agriculture. The conundrum was more difficult because, as James Allan observed, no private group wanting to found a university existed in Guelph. In the absence of any private support, all the costs for a university would fall on the government.[11]

The cabinet committee agreed, however, to inform the Guelph Advisory Board that the government was officially considering the proposal to create a university at Guelph. From now on the discussions would be formal. Civil servants from four departments — the treasury, public works, agriculture and education — were assigned to examine the facilities at Guelph and the costs of transforming them to university status. Both civil servants and officials at OAC were asked to study comparable American universities. No actual commitment was made, but the OAC board had every reason to feel optimistic in the fall of 1958. Even Premier Frost was contemplating the possibility of a university at Guelph, although this was not revealed publicly. His executive assistant wrote to the minister of agriculture after the premier reviewed the minutes of the cabinet committee's discussions on a possible university for Guelph:

> ... Mr. Frost said that he would go along with the suggestion that, at the appropriate time, a university be started at Guelph and that an Arts faculty be set up, with some of the present courses being transferred from OAC to the new Arts faculty ... On the other hand, as there seems to be no group at Guelph which might be interested in establishing a university, Mr. Frost wondered if the other possibility would be to make OAC a strictly agricultural college and to drop some of the other courses which do not strictly pertain to agriculture.[12]

Frost's ambivalence may well have influenced his minister of agriculture, because Goodfellow from then on was never wholeheartedly committed to university status for Guelph.

In the meantime, Dr. MacLachlan, encouraged by the signals of support from Queen's Park, had a personal timetable. He wanted the university at Guelph established by the beginning of the fall term, 1960. He briefed the Advisory Board in September on some of the implications. OAC, OVC and Macdonald Institute would retain their identity in the new university and they would be joined by three new colleges, one for arts and science, another for engineering and the third as a college to embrace all graduate studies. The campus, in addition, would house an Agricultural Research Institute. MacLachlan was confident this university could begin operations with the existing building facilities and faculty. Vigorous efforts would then be needed to acquire a new library, a humanities building and more residences to accommodate the new students. He advised the board to defer the admission of B.A. and M.A. students until the fall of 1963 when these additional facilities would be ready.

He also showed the board in draft form what a University Act might look like. He used the University of Toronto Act as a model for the clauses on the Board of Governors, Senate and the president. He and other board members understood the difficulties involved in describing the powers the board in an Ontario state university would have. There was no precedent to guide them.[13]

The board was pleased with the progress to date. Late in 1958, it authorized Dr. MacLachlan, Dr. Jones, Dr. McCready and Fred Presant, the chairman of the Advisory Board, to meet with the government as soon as possible to expedite a decision. The meeting could not be arranged until early February of the following year, when, armed with a new brief, the Guelph administrators presented their ideas to Allan, Goodfellow, and three key deputy ministers from the Departments of Agriculture, Education and Economics as well as the premier's executive assistant.

The brief reiterated the fact that a university at Guelph would help the province meet the demand for university places. But if the purpose was altruistic, the premises for university development at Guelph were unchanged from those advanced the previous summer. They still wanted the university at Guelph to be a provincial or state university with "a closer alliance to the Government of Ontario than obtains for the other provincial universities in Canada."[14] In contrast to other Ontario universities associated with urban centres, the Guelph campus would continue, as it had always done, to project its identity "to the rural area of Ontario as a whole." The status, objectives and the public recognition of the existing three institutions had to be enhanced and not jeopardized in any way. The organization sheets, included in the brief, were all based on the university continuing to remain within the fold of the Ontario Department of Agriculture.

William Goodfellow opened the meeting that day by saying the government's chief concern was to keep agriculture at the forefront at Guelph. Fred Presant echoed this comment, stressing the obligation to agriculture and reiterating the need to project an identity to Ontario's rural population. But he and his colleagues from Guelph wanted a commitment to action by the government. Presant said that on the campus "we have a partly completed university at the present time and we may as well be realistic and look to the future." The proposal to raise the status of the colleges to a university "should be carried out as soon as possible."[15]

At this point in the discussions, some of the underlying difficulties began to emerge. The deputy minister of economics, George Gathercole, a close confidant of Premier Frost, argued that if the Guelph colleges were to become a university, they should be treated on the same basis as other Ontario universities. He meant they should not receive special government subsidies because of their agricultural emphasis, and there must be community support behind the idea. James Allan directed a sharp barb at Guelph: "I doubt if there would be much community support from Guelph. They seem to have the feeling that the college supports them."

But Allan nevertheless strongly supported the idea of university status for his alma mater. He "expressed the feeling that the term 'Agricultural College' lacked prestige." Expanding OAC into a university would recapture the lost prestige, a desire Allan shared with many other OAC alumni.

With the other participants in the meeting anxious to give Guelph a green light in order to be ready to accommodate new students by September, 1960, George Gathercole continued to play the role of devil's advocate. "The institution could not be strictly rural and at the same time a cosmopolitan university. Some people thought Guelph too rural and some students might be lost by reason of this fact."

When Dr. MacLachlan stressed that the university "would be projected to all Ontario, it would be a state university responsible to the citizens as a whole," Gathercole asked him directly, "You would make it a provincial university?" MacLachlan replied, "yes." Gathercole, obviously taken aback at this presumption on the part of the Guelph colleges, said ominously "that the University of Toronto considered itself the Provincial University." For Gathercole, as for many others in the government and the Ontario university system, the ambition of OAC and its sister institutions to launch a state university as a rural counterpart to the University of Toronto was totally unrealistic.

Apparently sensing the meeting was running into difficulties, Allan resumed the momentum by again arguing the cost benefits of creating a university at Guelph. It would be cheaper there than at any other location in the province and by establishing a university at Guelph he, as provincial treasurer, would be relieved of some of the pressure he was facing to put money into universities elsewhere. The deputy ministers were delegated to prepare a report for cabinet and the Guelph representatives returned home naively confident that the logjam had been broken. Their confidence was misplaced.

Behind the scenes at Queen's Park, Premier Frost moved quietly to shelve the whole plan for the time being. Frost's actions, unknown to the Guelph administrators, scuttled the work the deputy ministers had been assigned to do and virtually left the Guelph proposals dangling in the wind.[16] Frost gave no reasons for his actions. He did not even confide in his cabinet ministers, but the premier's ever acute political nose apparently sensed this was not the time to proceed with a university for Guelph.

Premier Frost's actions coincided with the first sign of renewed pressure for university status by alumni. Alfred Hales, an OAC alumnus and the Conservative member of Parliament for Wellington South, noted with some concern the fund-raising efforts of Waterloo College in the Guelph area. The college sought $1,500,000 for its ambitious plans that would lead to the creation of the University of Waterloo. Hales wrote to the provincial minister of agriculture:

> The thought has occurred to me that, if this project is developed only fifteen miles from Guelph, it will have the tendency to interfere with the enlargement and development of the Ontario Agricultural College as a university. It is, I believe, quite conceivable that the powers that be would not want two universities so close together and naturally I feel that the OAC lends itself to the building of one of Ontario's finest universities.[17]

Hales was defending the local territory against neighbourhood poachers, but his loyal support of OAC had no immediate impact at Queen's Park. He didn't even receive a reply to his letter.

Within the Guelph colleges, the administrators patiently awaited a green light from the Ontario government, unaware of the premier's manoeuvring. They were even beginning the task of re-assuring the Ontario agricultural community that the conversion to university status "would not jeopardize in any way, the contributions to agriculture."[18] This was the message MacLachlan carried to the representatives of the Ontario livestock industry in May.

It took another chance meeting between MacLachlan and James Allan at the OAC Alumni Day in June, 1959 to inject some new energy into the bureaucratic process. Premier Frost's temporary injunction was lifted and now he was prepared at least to allow the discussions to continue. Allan convened another meeting of ministers, civil servants and President MacLachlan at Queen's Park at the end of June. This time "considerable enthusiasm" emerged for the Guelph scheme.[19] MacLachlan was instructed to draw up a draft University Act for the government to examine. He completed this task over the summer.

Rumours of changes at Guelph had now begun to percolate through the campus and the city. There was still no attempt to organize any formal community support or to embark on a campaign of private fund raising, but the *Guelph Daily Mercury* bestowed its editorial blessing on the possible transformation. "Guelph is justifiably proud of the Ontario Agricultural College and should it be raised to university status this will please every resident of the Royal City."[20]

By October, the Guelph documents were ready. Dr. MacLachlan had prepared two briefs that he presented to the Committee on University Affairs at Guelph on October 23.[21] One was a re-working of his February proposal explaining what the conversion to university status entailed. The purpose, as MacLachlan now described it, was to consolidate and integrate the existing facilities to achieve optimal operational efficiency. With degree-granting power, both undergraduate and graduate, the university would be able to cater to the needs of undergraduate students in agriculture, engineering and science (and later in arts) and embark on a more diversified program of graduate research in agriculture and veterinary medicine. He also proposed the creation of an Agricultural Research Institute with a budget separated from that of the university and responsible to its own council of directors.

His second brief was a draft act for the still nameless university. One key principle had remained unchanged. The first paragraph of the draft act specified that the university would be under the direct control of the Department of Agriculture of Ontario. Whatever the name, it was to be a state agricultural university. Following the meeting with the Committee on University Affairs, MacLachlan submitted a revised brief, incorporating his two earlier submissions in one document entitled "A University on the Guelph Campus." In this document he made the proposed Agricultural Research Institute responsible to the new university's Board of Governors and he spelled out once again the purpose of the new university: "Service to agriculture and to the rural youth of Ontario will remain the primary objective of the University."[22]

The Committee on University Affairs visited Guelph on October 23 to tour the campus and to hear the presentations by Dr. MacLachlan and his colleagues. Visiting the campus was a unique mark of favour from this committee since it did not make a practice of visiting any of the Ontario universities when carrying out its yearly reviews. The committee was created in 1958 by Premier Frost as an advisory committee to the government to evaluate either proposals from universities or plans for the establishment of new universities and to recommend funding to the minister of education. Because of the growing importance and cost of higher education in Ontario, the government required more specialized advice. From 1958 until December, 1960 when it was re-structured, the committee functioned strictly on a part-time basis and was composed primarily of civil servants, who were experts in economics or accounting. The chairman was C.F. Canon, the chief director of education, and the other principal members were George Gathercole, the deputy minister of economics; H.H. Walker, the education department's chief accountant; and H. H. Cotnam, provincial auditor. The secretary was J. R. McCarthy, then the superintendent of curriculum in the Department of Education.[23] Because these men were very busy with their other heavy departmental responsibilities, they had little time to give to educational issues and certainly they could not carry out a continuous overseeing responsibility.

The Guelph administrators were very pleased with the outcome of the meeting at the campus on October 23 and believed with reason that the key Ontario civil servants who had inspected the facilities and had heard the presentation were impressed with Guelph and would report favourably to the government. The committee met again in Toronto and struck a sub-committee that had another meeting with MacLachlan and then sent a report to Premier Frost. Prophetically, the date was Friday, November 13. MacLachlan, summarizing all his discussions with government officials for the Joint Advisory Committees, concluded that he was very optimistic about meeting his timetable for conversion to university status by the fall of 1960.[24] He, too, was unaware of hidden obstacles at Queen's Park.

What actually happened to the 1959 proposal to create a state university from OAC, OVC and Macdonald Institute is not completely clear from the existing historical records. What is evident is that Premier Frost and his government decided not to proceed with the idea in 1959. But this decision came after he had publicly announced the government's intention to establish three new universities, one at Sault Ste. Marie, one at Sudbury and one at Guelph. Frost made this announcement at the opening of a new dentistry building at the University of Toronto in November, 1959.[25] The government clearly got cold feet at the last minute, but precisely why may never be known. Certainly the main participants at Guelph were never told.

When the Committee on University Affairs met in Toronto later in 1959 to discuss the Guelph proposals, George Gathercole dominated the meeting. One of his colleagues said of Gathercole: "He saw himself as a person who was very close to the Premier and was free to comment on anything in any department to Frost."[26] In this instance, Gathercole seized the initiative from the civil servants in both the Departments of Education and Agriculture and subjected the prospective Guelph university to an exacting analysis. The alternatives as he saw them were to continue the *status quo* and raise the fees for non-farmers or to go further and establish a university with an arts faculty. He explored the repercussions of each alternative, particularly the financial ones. How much would a university at Guelph cost the Ontario government? Would there be any savings? What difficulties would arise? He was particularly troubled by the idea of the government supporting arts students at Guelph at the same level as agricultural students. He noted caustically that if a university was to be built at Guelph, the local people should be required to give financial backing.[27]

His questions formed the background to the memorandum Gathercole wrote on behalf of the Committee on University Affairs for the premier after Frost's announcement that Guelph would be one of three new universities the province intended to start. Gathercole suggested two alternative plans for Frost, "both of which would be a distinct improvement over the present position."[28] The first alternative was to maintain OAC, OVC and Macdonald Institute as government colleges, but with a stronger central organization to operate all of them together and an Ontario Agricultural Research Foundation "which would conduct a broader and more intensified program of research into all phases of the agricultural industry ..." Under this plan, fees would be increased for all students to help offset government costs.

Gathercole then laid out what he saw as the advantages and disadvantages of this alternative. The main advantage was its simplicity. There would be relatively few changes required and it would allay suspicions among farmers that agriculture was becoming too academic. Gathercole identified one other advantage: "students who meet the proper requirements may graduate with a University of Toronto degree."

But there were some important disadvantages in retaining the *status quo*:

> It does not afford as good an opportunity for advanced work as does a full-fledged university, nor does graduation from it have the same broad prestige as it would have if it were such a university. Agriculture is becoming increasingly complex and variegated, requiring more specialization and the application of technology and science. To provide the courses in the present curriculum requires highly qualified and specialized staff. This staff can probably be used more fully, more economically and to better advantage if there is a balanced university program. Similarly, university status would make possible the engagement of more

specialized teachers and thus open to those primarily interested in agriculture direct contacts that would not otherwise be available.

The second alternative Gathercole advanced was to create a university at Guelph in which the agriculture program would be funded directly by a separate provincial grant. He identified three advantages in university status:

1. The Ontario Agricultural College is located in a prosperous part of Ontario, surrounded by expanding areas of population and industry.
2. It already has a well-established reputation as one of the foremost agricultural and veterinary colleges in the world and it has gathered to itself a reputable staff readily capable of expansion.
3. The development of general university courses at Guelph would help to meet some of the requirements of the avalanche of students who will be seeking to enter university over the next 10-20 years and moderate the pressure on the facilities of other universities.

Against these three advantages of location, reputation and the assistance in meeting the onrush of university students, Gathercole set three significant disadvantages:

1. There does not seem to be much local interest in the development of the Ontario Agricultural College as a university. Financed in the past almost exclusively by the Province, the Ontario Agricultural College has not attracted to itself the type of local interest which has been such a major and favourable factor in the development of the University of Western Ontario, McMaster and others. To make Plan Two successful, there should be a strong municipal and area interest in the university and a willingness on the part of local authorities and citizens to support the university through their financial contributions and enthusiastic voluntary participation in its work.

Gathercole pointed out the salary and pension administration problems involved in transforming the three colleges into a university.

2. In our view, if the Ontario Agricultural College is to be developed as a university, then, except for the agricultural school or faculty, it should be prepared to accept the same conditions of operation as other universities.

3. There may be some feeling of distrust in rural Ontario that the College is departing from its strict preoccupation with matters agricultural, veterinary and rural.

Having carefully balanced the advantages and disadvantages of the two plans, Gathercole was equally careful in his conclusion. He and the committee of civil servants did not favour one over the other. Instead, they offered a brief neutral summary of the two options:

Obviously Plan Two is more ambitious and radical than Plan One. With Plan One there would be fewer dislocations and perhaps less disquiet among farm groups who wish to guard its future as a practical agricultural institution. On the other hand, Plan Two offers more scope, provides more opportunity for study, research and work in the more advanced fields of agriculture and the related sciences. In the end the university's reputation would be broadened and extended.[29]

Gathercole and his fellow civil servants did make one definite recommendation. Whichever plan the government adopted, they advocated the creation of an Ontario Agricultural Research Foundation to consolidate and integrate agricultural research.

We believe that Ontario's agricultural industry must be geared to meeting the challenges of foreign imports of agricultural products. The creation of an Ontario Agricultural Research Foundation such as we have suggested, properly organized, would go a long way toward overcoming some of the handicaps of climate and economic scale that exist in our Province and toward meeting the competition from the United States and abroad that is increasing yearly.[30]

Early in December, the *London Free Press* carried a historical sketch of OAC under the headline, "Soon to be elevated to University Status."[31] The *Free Press*, along with people in the Guelph colleges and across the province, had taken the premier's announcement at face value and it offered its readers some background on what would be western Ontario's newest university. One of the statements in the article was both prophetic and historical. "Politics has always played a dominant role in the fortunes of the provincially-controlled college."

One of the people who read the *Free Press* article was J.D. MacLachlan, and he read it with great concern. He wrote to the minister of agriculture the following day, enclosing both the article and a resolution passed by the Joint Advisory Committee of the three colleges at their meeting on November 27.[32] MacLachlan wanted an authoritative statement from the Department of Agriculture to show that a university at Guelph would enhance agriculture in the province, not jeopardize it. The resolution asked the minister to release the studies and proposals for the university to reassure the rural public of the province. One of the effects of the premier's announcement about Guelph was to awaken latent fears that OAC would be reduced in status within a university and Ontario's farmers would suffer as a result. Those farmers saw OAC as the flagship of the Department of Agriculture and their rural votes were the solid base of Conservative party support. Leslie Frost was not about to take any action to risk that rural support, and the very mention of the danger may have been enough to cause him to set aside the plan for a state university at Guelph.

The 1959 Guelph proposal was not formally or publicly rejected. That was not the government's way. Open rejection might have caused an angry reaction. Instead, in the words of the secretary to the Committee on University Affairs, "nothing was done about it." The Guelph people "weren't turned down, but they were not encouraged." What happened to the proposal? It was filed and "died of malnutrition."[33]

It was an exasperating time for both J.D. MacLachlan and Trevor Lloyd Jones who visited Toronto regularly, seeking to expedite a decision. MacLachlan recalled it "as the most frustrating period in my entire career." He never did get a meeting with the premier. William Goodfellow, the minister of agriculture, "wouldn't say no." MacLachlan returned from repeated meetings in Toronto, "feeling as if I was in a fog. I had nothing to put my fingers on and grab."[34] Trevor Lloyd Jones has similar memories. "Doug and I would go down to Toronto, just the two of us, to see the minister, who couldn't seem to care less about the subject."[35] Indifference prevailed. The two Guelph men, unable to talk to the premier, were foiled in their efforts to get their message across at the highest level of the provincial government. The plan they had worked so hard on was quietly buried in ministerial files. Guelph would have to wait five more years for its university.

CHAPTER 3

Federating the Colleges

Once the university proposal of 1959 had been quietly pigeonholed by Leslie Frost and his government, the idea of university status for the Guelph colleges faded into the background for the next four years, finally resurfacing in early 1963. In the meantime, another proposal—actually a new version of an old idea—emerged to occupy the attention of faculty and students on the campus — the federation of the three institutions under a central administrative apparatus. In 1962, this consolidation became a reality when the Federated Colleges Act passed the Ontario Legislature, the first major administrative change to occur in the forty years since the Ontario Veterinary College moved to Guelph.

The federation plan was a direct outgrowth of a management consultant study of the operations of the three colleges, ordered by the Department of Agriculture and undertaken early in 1960 by Woods Gordon and Company. The department ordered the study because it believed the colleges could be administered more efficiently. When the study began, its authors thought of presenting their ideas for an integrated campus either as a university or as a federation of the three colleges. The completed study opted for federating the three colleges, a solution that was in line with the views of the key officials in the Department of Agriculture and the beliefs of William Goodfellow and President MacLachlan. The two men, however, approached the issue from diametrically opposed positions. MacLachlan saw federation as a stepping stone to university status, while Goodfellow regarded it as a convenient way of avoiding the university question altogether. The Woods Gordon study fashioned a blueprint for the new structure, which the report hinted would be flexible enough to handle a considerable expansion in student numbers if required. The federation would be administered by a president and the three deans of the existing colleges, who would report to the president. Woods Gordon also gave the government a detailed analysis of all the changes required in personnel and management as well as suggestions on such routine administrative matters as accounting and business procedures.[1]

J. D. MacLachlan had already advocated the federation of the colleges in a lengthy letter to the minister of agriculture at the end of February, 1960.[2] He had reluctantly accepted that it was not politically expedient for the government to raise the colleges to university level, and he fell back upon the older plan of federation as an interim solution until the right moment came to create a university. MacLachlan believed that if a federation was in place, the government could easily transform the institution into a university by renaming it and investing it with the appropriate authority. The federation therefore would function as an embryonic university especially if it received degree-granting powers of its own, an option MacLachlan also sought. An additional and strong attraction of a federation, as he pointed out to Goodfellow, was that it would "leave no avenue for distrust or enigmatic reaction on the part of our farm public." MacLachlan wanted at all costs to avoid another rural backlash.

In an interview, J.D. MacLachlan reiterated that federation "was a necessary step before we got the university." It enabled the consolidation of the budgets of the three colleges and the creation of one library from the three previous ones. With it came greater administrative efficiency, which he believed was a necessary preliminary to university status.[3] Not all of MacLachlan's colleagues in OAC agreed on the importance of federation as a necessary prerequisite to university status. One remembers that "it seemed to me that it was an administrative convenience we were talking about."[4]

MacLachlan's enthusiasm for the concept of federation was not shared by Trevor Lloyd Jones who remembers it as "MacLachlan's baby." Jones went along with the idea without being happy at some of its consequences. He felt there was no basis for the contention that the provincial government had to have more co-ordination over the expenditure of funds and he viewed the integration of academic and administrative services in each college as positive rather than inefficient. But, in this issue, as in all others affecting the relationship of the Guelph institutions to the provincial government, OVC and its principal played a supporting role. The lead belonged to OAC whose president was now convinced federation was the means to achieve a university.

Other observers were not nearly as optimistic that the government scheme for a management study of the operations of the colleges would lead eventually to university status. Commenting on the minister's announcement of the appointment of Woods Gordon to do the review, *Guelph Daily Mercury's* columnist Verne McIlwraith concluded, "apparently there is little hope of the Guelph colleges taking on university status for some time, if ever."[5] Although his pessimism turned out to be exaggerated, he had correctly gauged the intentions of the Frost government. Reorganization to achieve greater efficiency, not greater autonomy leading to university status, remained the government's aim.

Another issue that had arisen in connection with federation was the question of agricultural research. For MacLachlan, retaining control of research within the college was as important as the consolidation of the administration of the three colleges and the acquisition of degree-granting powers. Agricultural research was just as vital from the perspective of the provincial government, but MacLachlan and the government differed greatly over how it should be carried out. MacLachlan's university proposal of November, 1959 had envisaged a research institute as an integral part of the university, accountable to the university's board of governors. The Advisory Committee on University Affairs recommended the creation of an agricultural research institute without specifying who would control it. By 1960, when MacLachlan wrote to the minister about federating the colleges, rumours were prevalent that a separate agricultural research institute would be created, removing the control of research from the OAC and placing it within the Department of Agriculture.

MacLachlan was adamant in his opposition to such an idea, viewing research and academic teaching as "integral functions of the campus as a whole." He argued that at no time in the past had research in the departments within OAC and OVC been as well integrated as it was then. He warned the minister in eloquent language of the dangers of separating research from an academic environment and placing it under a director who was accountable only to the minister:

> Research is a unique endeavour in which the research specialist must have full freedom to use his own training, experience, acumen and ingenuity in solving an unknown. No one is mentally equipped to mastermind the procedure for all the individual research projects within this complex panorama of agricultural problems. Furthermore, the chain of administrative authority over any man must not encompass a diversification which leads to confusion if not

stultification—no man will effectively serve under two masters.[6]

Worse still in MacLachlan's mind was the prospect of a separate agricultural research facility without the federation of the colleges. MacLachlan pushed hard for two principles in the prospective reorganization: the consolidation of the campus organization and the full integration of research within the Guelph campus. What was not said in this letter, but was also preying on MacLachlan's mind, was that more than 70 per cent of the OAC budget and 60 per cent of the OVC budget went to agricultural research, services and extension. Removing this from the administrative control of the colleges could have a serious impact on their operations.

The Woods Gordon study identified the sums spent on research and proposed federating the three institutions. When the government received the study, it referred it, as it had previous proposals, to the Committee on University Affairs for examination. The committee devoted four meetings during the summer and early autumn of 1960 to a full review of the Woods Gordon document. It agreed that a general reorganization of the administrative structure was needed and spent some time haggling over how much the fees at the colleges should be increased. By September, the committee was finally prepared to make some definite recommendations to the government on the three major questions confronting it. Should the Woods Gordon reorganization be accepted? Should the affiliation of the Guelph colleges with the University of Toronto cease? Should a vice-president for research and extension be created within a reorganized administration? The committee's conclusions were that the federation of the colleges should be accepted, but affiliation with the University of Toronto should not be broken for the time being. The committee also favoured the appointment of a senior academic responsible to the president to take charge of research and graduate studies.[7]

When the committee made its recommendations in September, the members had in front of them a draft act to federate the colleges, prepared by J.D. MacLachlan himself and sent to the minister of agriculture at the end of July. To MacLachlan, the act entailed a "minimal change from the current system of operation." Each of the existing colleges would retain its name and identity. MacLachlan stressed repeatedly that his proposed act "encompasses nothing to occasion consternation on the part of the agricultural public" and even suggested that the cutting of ties with the University of Toronto, and subsequent bringing of all aspects of the colleges' operations under the control of the Department of Agriculture, should "in itself more than nullify any consternation among the agricultural community."[8]

Goodfellow made sure Premier Frost saw MacLachlan's draft act and accompanying letter. He endorsed MacLachlan's suggestions and displayed the same sensitivity to potential hostility from rural Ontario. "By federating the three existing faculties rather than indicating that other faculties might be established, the Government would be relieved of any criticism we might get from the farm element that agriculture was being pushed to one side."[9]

It was not consternation among the agricultural public that stopped the federated colleges obtaining their own degree-granting powers, although exaggerated fears of a reaction among the rural community to any changes at OAC still permeated Queen's Park. The civil servants sitting on the Committee on University Affairs and, in particular, George Gathercole, opposed giving the Guelph colleges the authority to grant their own degrees. Gathercole argued that since all the costs were paid by the Department of Agriculture, other universities would not accept the idea of one degree-granting institution being treated more generously than all the others. For Gathercole, the economist, this was a major impediment to degree-granting autonomy. The academic supervision exercised in name, although not in fact by the University of Toronto, preserved a fiction of tutelage that would continue for several more years.

It took another month following the September meeting of the Committee of University Affairs for its report to be circulated to all the relevant government departments, and even by the beginning of the new year no action had occurred on the recommendations. Some of the key participants met with the minister of agriculture early in 1961, but there were still misunderstandings between the earlier proposals for full university status and the newer concept of federation.[10] Eventually, it appeared that the federation plan could proceed and the solicitor of the Department of Agriculture began the actual work of drafting the necessary legislation. By January 23, 1961 he had identified seventeen points he felt the minister had to resolve before the task could be completed.

The first, symptomatic of the degree of confusion within the civil service over the nature of the institution to be created, was its name. C.W. Caskey, the solicitor, suggested it should be called The University of Guelph because two of the three colleges were not strictly agricultural. The suggestion was premature and the solicitor had to be instructed on just what the minister had in mind. Another complication occurred because both the Ontario Agricultural College and the Ontario Veterinary College had been created by acts of the Ontario Legislature, but Macdonald Institute had not. The solicitor was not certain what its status in law was. The most difficult question, however, was how the federated colleges were to be governed.

Caskey delicately pointed out how far the Guelph colleges had developed. They had "expanded beyond the point where the control should be exercised by the minister alone." He had stopped his work of drafting the bill because he had been unable to resolve "the particularly troublesome point" of "whether or not the entire set-up at the federated colleges would continue to be under the direction and control of the minister of agriculture. It appears to me that if such is the case there is little function that can be given to a Board of Governors."[11] The solicitor was not the only person to have trouble with the question of whether the real authority lay in the governing body or with the government.

Caskey's memorandum temporarily blocked further progress on the bills, but Goodfellow formally presented the reorganization plan to Premier Frost. The premier was not really interested in the legalities that had arisen within the Department of Agriculture. Instead, he was preoccupied by the implications of the institutions' budgets, which he suspected were out of control. He wrote a revealing letter to C.A. Cotnam, provincial auditor, suggesting the need for a "good, hard-boiled controller" appointed by the government to discover what was really happening at Guelph. For comparison purposes, Frost placed the nearly $7,800,000 going to the Guelph colleges against the $1,475,000 appropriated for Queen's University. Then he explained why he found the figures so alarming:

> Of course, the trend is to make these federated colleges into a university. Just imagine the effect if these estimates were translated into the estimates of the Department of Education and placed against those we are providing for Queen's, Western, McMaster, Assumption, Toronto, etc., etc. Either we would have to cut the federated colleges down to size, or else our university bill would go up to at least $100 million.[12]

Frost was very skeptical that the federation bill would give any answers or help the government to resolve its dilemma. How could a board of governors appointed by the government tell the government how to spend its money? Frost confessed that he had not been impressed with the Woods Gordon report:

> which rather took the position that we were running a university up there anyway and that we might as well give it the necessary status. They were not, however, asked to appraise what our position would be with the other universities. One of the great problems with OAC is that we are giving virtually a university course to all sorts of young

people who have no relation to agriculture at all and come from Hamilton and Toronto.[13]

The following day the premier again discussed the OAC question with the minister of agriculture, the provincial auditor and Gathercole, the deputy minister of economics. From this meeting came the tentative decision to separate the research funds from the OAC estimates and place them under an agricultural research branch or institute separately accountable to the minister of agriculture. This, said the premier, "then would allow us to deal with OAC and the other colleges on their merits and try and devise ways and means of getting the matter under some control and direction."[14] Frost's action stalled the federation bill until the government decided to proceed with the creation of an agricultural research institute. J.R. McCarthy, who served during this time as secretary to the Committee on University Affairs, remembers that Leslie Frost's attitude towards universities in this era was very much influenced by his experience as provincial treasurer.[15] This emerged very plainly in Frost's consideration of proposals affecting OAC.

By the end of May, 1961, the minister of agriculture again pressed the premier for action on the reorganization of the Guelph colleges. Now Goodfellow echoed the arguments Frost had used earlier:

> Since becoming Minister of Agriculture, I have had a growing concern over this situation due to the fact that the budget for the three Colleges has now reached eight million dollars per year, and there has been a tendency on the part of some people at Guelph to develop empires and, as faculty members, to resent to some extent what they consider to be political interference. In reality our concern is for the judicious expenditure of public funds and at the same time to keep pace with the needs of modern agricultural technology in teaching, research and extension.[16]

Goodfellow wanted Frost's permission to establish an agricultural research institute with a director who would report directly to the minister of agriculture. The institute would co-ordinate all the agricultural research at Guelph, amounting to almost half of the $8 million appropriation. Goodfellow told the premier that once the research funds had been separated from the money required for teaching, the government could then proceed with the next step of integrating the institutions themselves. Frost approved the plan and also the appointment of D. N. Huntley, head of the Field Husbandry Department at OAC, as the first director. His approval came with a cautionary word to his minister of agriculture to maintain the farmers' support:

> I am sure that you will keep the various farm organiza-
> tions informed so that they will feel that they are taking a
> part in this, and will not feel that changes are being made
> at OAC that will go to the detriment of the farmer.[17]

The premier had decided that no reorganization of the colleges could take place until the agricultural research had been separated from the colleges and placed under the control of a government-run agricultural research institute. His shrewd political insight had also glimpsed the possibility of extra political credit to be gained from a research institute. He believed the government was not reaping any political benefit from the agricultural research being carried out at Guelph. From this strictly political perspective, the separation of research was a desirable goal.

Early in July, 1961, Goodfellow issued a press release announcing the creation of the institute and Huntley's appointment as director. The announcement proclaimed some far-reaching benefits for Ontario agriculture. The institute would help the province work closely with private corporations on research projects and foster closer co-operation in agricultural research between the provincial and federal governments. Goodfellow also claimed the change was part of the administrative reorganization of OAC, OVC and Macdonald Institute that would pave the way for a university at Guelph.[18]

The public announcement was disingenuous to say the least. Neither the Department of Agriculture nor its minister had any intention in June, 1961 of raising the Guelph colleges to university status. The real purpose of the new institute was to bring the budgets for agricultural research at Guelph under much closer government control and to ensure maximum political impact of the results of agricultural research. J.D. MacLachlan had been unsuccessful in trying to persuade the Ontario government to leave agricultural research under academic control. Political imperatives were too strong. Research, however, would still be carried on within the OAC. MacLachlan's task now was to ensure a harmonious working relationship between the OAC and the agricultural research institute.

While the government had been wrestling with the future of the colleges, isolated voices—mainly OAC alumni—kept up the public and private pressure for university status. Dr. J.R. Weir, the dean of agriculture at the University of Manitoba and a former OAC faculty member, delivered the J.J. Morrison memorial lecture to a large audience at OAC in November, 1960. He carefully stressed "the advantage of agriculture and other professional faculties being part of a university, rather than separate, isolated colleges."[19] He also told his audience in remarks obviously meant for the government's ear that universities had more academic freedom. Weir's message was that Ontario should follow Manitoba's example. Weir acted as a willing stalking horse for the OAC faculty who had invited him. Ralph Campbell, then the head of the Agricultural Economics Department, said that he and his colleagues working for university status "chose other people to fire the bullets we had been working on in Guelph."[20]

Weir's speech found a sympathetic echo among the students. The student newspaper reported it in detail and added a front page editorial reinforcing his conclusions:

> All too often we have been exposed to arguments on why Agriculture should remain separate from a university. It was time that the other side of the argument was presented ...
>
> Agricultural students usually are strongly biased towards technical subjects and specific agricultural problems. This is too narrow a base for sound education. In a university these biases can be modified through contact with students and staff in social sciences and humanities .... The emphasis in too many courses here is mistakenly placed on learning specific details when the emphasis should be on teaching students how to think ...

The editorial defended the need for complete academic freedom at the colleges and concluded:

> If our campus is to become part of a university environment it is obvious that a university will have to be founded in Guelph. We cannot go to Toronto. University status would free us from our very apparent "narrowness" and political control.[21]

The Rural Co-operator, the official organ of the Ontario Federation of Agriculture, also reported Weir's speech and supported him with a trenchant editorial, arguing for an independent university at Guelph:

> The association of an arts college in federation with the agricultural and veterinary colleges would be good for all concerned and it seems to us to make more sense, when additional universities are needed, to expand OAC where

land and administrators are available, than to start from scratch in some other location ...

It seems to us ridiculous to expect OAC faculty members to adhere to civil service hours and holiday schedules when their counterparts at universities are free to plan their work, study and research on the basis of the university year.[22]

The *Co-operator's* report and editorial became political weapons in the legislature the following March during the debate on the agricultural estimates. Gordon Innes, the Liberal MPP from Oxford and an OAC alumnus, used both the report of the speech and the editorial to buttress his demand for university status to be given to the Guelph colleges "to upgrade agriculture and farming" in Ontario. Student opinion, too, was solidifying in favour of university status. A columnist in the student newspaper echoed the voices being heard in the legislature. "It is time that the politicians got out, and the OAC became an independent university."[23]

The government had also received private representations from at least one Conservative. William Newman, a defeated Progressive Conservative candidate in the 1959 provincial election, who would later serve as minister of agriculture and food, wrote to Goodfellow after discussing the future of OAC with several fellow alumni in Durham. "We feel, as I am sure that your department does, that it would be a very fine thing to have the College on the Hill a full fledged University."[24]

The government, led by the premier, was very careful in the way it deflected these representations even though at that time it had no intention of meeting the demands. To Conservative supporters like Newman, the government announced its plan of federating the colleges to bring more efficient administration. To the opposition, Frost offered the traditional Conservative defence of OAC. It was a farmers' college and a place for agricultural research. But he also referred to one of the questions that had bedevilled the consideration of university status for Guelph. How could the government continue to subsidize agricultural education without subsidizing non-agricultural education at the same high level? When another Liberal challenged the minister of agriculture to have the colleges incorporated under the Department of Education, he received a sharp retort to go out and talk to the farmers of Ontario before making suggestions like that. Goodfellow reiterated the premier's position. OAC was the farmers' school. Leslie Frost's government was not about to tamper with a cornerstone of its rural support.[25] The prevailing political perception of the Guelph institutions at Queen's Park until the early 1960s was a major obstacle in the way of any fundamental change.

At the very time the government decided to create the Agricultural Research Institute, Ralph Campbell, head of the Agricultural Economics Department, voiced concerns shared by a number of his colleagues. Ralph Campbell was a veteran who attended university in the heady post-war days. After graduating from the University of Toronto, Campbell went to Oxford in 1949 as a Rhodes Scholar and then joined the OAC Agricultural Economics Department in 1951 as a lecturer. He contemplated leaving after only six months, but when he told President MacLachlan of his intentions he suddenly found himself made professor and head of the department. As Campbell himself recalled, "You can imagine the meteoric rise that was. I had a B.A. from Toronto and a B.A. from Oxford and I had never taken a course in Agricultural Economics." By 1961 he had succeeded in building a very strong undergraduate and extension program as well as establishing close connections with Ontario's farm community. Campbell remembers that "we all regarded them out there as our constituency somehow. Almost everybody on the staff it seemed came from a farm and that had a very important role in making people very acceptable back in the farming community."[26]

Campbell always felt the lack of the broadening influences only a university could bring. After a number of years of pushing for a university, he wrote a paper in 1961 entitled "OAC at the Crossroads." He sent it to key civil servants in the Department of Agriculture who, in turn, made sure it reached the minister's desk. The ideas he advanced were similar to the arguments J.D. MacLachlan used. Agriculture in Ontario faced some momentous challenges and "the biggest in the long run is the way the Ontario Agricultural College will develop."[27] OAC faced two alternative routes, stated Campbell:

> On the one hand it can become a bona fide university with freedom to undertake research, to write, and to speak, in a free and uninhibited fashion on the problems of today and even more important, on the problems of the future; or on the other hand it can become nothing more than a subsidiary of the Ontario Department of Agriculture with close supervision and control by the Ontario government.[28]

Because OAC faculty had always performed "a dual role" as faculty members and civil servants, they were constrained, especially in research. "Always lurking in the background, however, has been the possibility that research, articles and speeches which were contrary to the present interests of the provincial government would be met with the subtle forms of disapproval ... failure to promote and failure to grant additional funds." Campbell, who had experienced political criticism of his own work, strongly believed that an agricultural research institute under the direct control of the department would only perpetuate what he felt was an unsatisfactory situation. The areas of research, what results should be published, and the emphasis on particular areas of research all would be affected by political pressures and subtle but powerful forms of censorship. But if the research institute was part of an independent university, "all the benefits of planning and co-ordination may be obtained without threat to academic freedom and danger of political interference." Unlike agricultural extension work, research thrived in a different administrative atmosphere, where freedom of thought and personal initiative were stimulated.

Having criticized the establishment of an agricultural research institute which had already been approved, he offered his own forthright conclusion to the alternatives he had posed. OAC had to go "in the direction of an independent university as in the other five Canadian colleges of agriculture, and not in the direction of a subsidiary directly controlled by the Ontario Department of Agriculture."[29]

Campbell's paper was also a signal of the frustration that led to his decision to leave OAC. Years later he concluded that "if there had been a really strong indication in 1961 when I was making up my mind that there would be a university here with a Faculty of Arts and a Board of Governors that was free of government intervention, I would have stayed on." Once he decided to leave, he had an interview with William Stewart, the minister of agriculture, and told him, "the reason I was leaving was that I thought it was going to be too many years before OAC-OVC would become a university. I wanted to be at a university and I wanted the independence, freedom and the opportunity to study anything we wanted to study without looking over our shoulders to see if someone was nodding approval or shaking his head and frowning."[30] Campbell went on to a distinguished academic career, first at the University of Toronto where he was associate dean of arts and science and principal of Scarborough College, and then at the University of Manitoba where he served five years as president.

Neither the representations from inside OAC, or those from outside, had any immediate success in altering the course the Frost government charted, and the Robarts government continued during its first year of office. One of the ironies of the many promises made by Premier Frost and Goodfellow, his minister of agriculture, about imminent changes at Guelph was that when Leslie Frost resigned as premier in November, 1961, no legislation had yet appeared to implement any of these commitments. John Robarts appointed a younger and more energetic man as minister of agriculture. W.A. Stewart soon shuffled the senior civil servants in the department. This new team introduced the legislation for both the Agricultural Research Institute and the Federated Colleges little more than a month after they took office.

As Stewart recalled, this legislation was not seen at the time as radical, nor was it intended to lead right away to university status:

> We were all new in that Government and we were some-
> what reluctant to just rush out and take three old estab-
> lished institutions such as these were, with a worldwide
> reputation, and chuck them into a University without
> knowing really what would happen. I think there was a
> general reluctance along that line.[31]

The first Speech from the Throne of the Robarts government on November 22, 1961 announced the intention to introduce legislation to set up an agriculture research institute "to co-ordinate" agricultural research in Ontario and initiate changes to the three colleges "to produce greater efficiency and economy."[32] Less than a month later, on December 11, 1961, Bills 49 and 50 were given first reading in the legislature. By treating the bills together, the Robarts government acknowledged that both pieces of legislation were designed to bring significant changes to the Guelph campus.

The two bills were referred to the Legislature's Standing Committee on Agriculture for examination. In documents prepared for the committee, the department reaffirmed its goals of integrating the educational programs through federation and separating the research and educational costs through the device of an agricultural research institute. The accounting confusion, which had frustrated repeated efforts to change the administrative structure and was a primary reason for the creation of the institute, was highlighted.

> In essence a very extensive agricultural research station
> is being operated in conjunction with the educational
> programs, a combination that has been a constant source
> of misunderstanding when attempts are made to prorate
> facilities and operational costs against student
> population.[33]

As well as a clearer identification of research costs, the institute's role was to develop a program of agricultural research to maintain Ontario's competitiveness in an increasingly tough North American and world market.

In the eyes of department officials, Bill 50, establishing the Agricultural Research Institute, was an innovative step to highlight the importance of agricultural research. They defended Bill 49, which federated the three Guelph colleges, in more conservative terms. The colleges (Macdonald Institute was now to become a college) retained "their well-established names" and no basic changes occurred in the programs they offered or in their relationship to the government. MPPs were told it was "significant" that the deputy minister of agriculture would serve on the Board of Regents as an *ex-officio* member. He would be the channel of control from Queen's Park, confirmation that federating the colleges would not make them independent. Faculty members would still be civil servants. On these fundamental points the proposed change was cosmetic rather than real.

The premier made this explicit in the Legislature before the bills were formally considered in committee. When challenged by Robert Nixon, the Liberal MPP from Brant, as to why the colleges were not being given university status, Robarts replied that the colleges existed "for the benefit of the agricultural community of the province" and did not fit into the pattern of the province's universities. The universities, he stated, were independent and had sources of revenue apart from government funds, while the colleges were completely subsidized. He also raised the question of the duplication of facilities with universities in London, Windsor, and Waterloo. "... It is a good question as to whether we need another general university in the Guelph area."[34] Robarts concluded "that this is basically a farmers' college and has been over the years." He foresaw no immediate likelihood of university status, although federation and the separation of agricultural research were, he argued, steps in that direction.

The Standing Committee on Agriculture took the opportunity offered by its examination of the two bills to visit Guelph in 1962 and tour the institutions. Twenty members of the legislature made the trip and had a two-hour meeting with college officials. When the committee met a second time to consider the bills, only one item of either bill proved at all controversial. This was the makeup of the Board of Regents. MacLachlan had suggested a board of regents rather than a board of governors to avoid the implication that this board would usurp any of the government's powers. He took the name from one of the recommendations, endorsed by the legislature, of the report of a Select Committee of the Ontario Legislature in 1950, which favoured federation. Apparently, no one on the select committee was interested in the powers of the Board of Regents, but Liberal members tried to ensure a strong voice for alumni by moving an amendment that three members be nominated by the alumni and be alumni themselves. The government majority easily defeated this attempt and both bills passed without any major changes.[35]

The OAC students had also tried in vain to amend the bill. George Greenlees, president of the Student Union Council, wrote to Everett Biggs, the deputy minister of agriculture, early in March supporting the idea of federation but strongly protesting the name to be given to the new institution, "The Federated Colleges of the Department of Agriculture."[36] Greenlees claimed the name "will be detrimental to the development of the institutions and to the students and graduates that leave the institution during the time the name is in force." The council was not prepared to back down in its campaign. In the autumn after the bill had been formally proclaimed, a motion passed in a union council meeting formally proscribing the use of the name "Federated Colleges" by any student organization on campus. The name was "a verbal monstrosity" that cast a stigma on all the students and graduates of the three colleges.[37]

By the fall there were other signs of discontent and indications that federation had whetted appetites for university status instead of deflecting them. The lead article in the student paper of September 26, 1962 captured a sense of the disillusionment felt on the campus.

> A year ago when it became apparent that the three colleges on this campus were to be united under one administration, many faculty members and students believed that at last this campus was awakening from many years of dormancy and that indeed this would be the first step towards university status. However, now that this unification has arrived it is evident that we still are to remain under political control and that indeed we are no closer to a university charter. Many people, myself included, view the federation as a step backward and believe it "to be an utter farce."

The writer, Jon Church, went on to argue that unless the three colleges became a university they would cease to exist as institutions of higher learning. Church, like many other students and faculty, deeply resented the direct political control exercised by Queen's Park. "The administration finds itself unable to introduce any important programs without first phoning a man at Queen's Park and seeking his approval on matters he knows little about ... outside of how it will affect the votes at the next election."[38]

J.D. MacLachlan, who had been named president of the Federated Colleges, carefully clipped this article and sent it to the deputy minister of agriculture along with another clipping indicating that the local NDP riding association had passed a resolution endorsing university status. One of the major planks in the resolution was the need for academic freedom.

> A university staff has the advantage of academic freedom and an opportunity to express independent thought so essential for objective work free of the electoral desires of a ministry whose very existence might discourage the production and the transmission of information vital to the community as a whole and to agriculture in particular. It would also be free from the rules of a civil service which are incompatible with the traditional way of life of academic institutions.[39]

Officials in the Department of Agriculture were anxious to do what they could to ensure that the new federation got off to a good start and they were clearly unprepared for the criticism that had emerged. Deputy Minister Everett Biggs asked the department's solicitor for a report on possible changes to the act to give the Guelph colleges degree-granting powers and to find a different name. The solicitor discouraged him from making any changes. "The name 'Federated Colleges' appears throughout the Act in so many places that an act to make the necessary amendments would be longer than the present act."[40]

Biggs also made sure his minister was aware of the Guelph feelings. As deputy minister and an OAC alumnus, Biggs favoured degree-granting status for the colleges as a measure to enhance their prestige and to head off the growing clamour for a university.

> At the present moment, and no doubt in the coming months, it is apparent that there will be continuing pressure for university status at Guelph. This pressure will come from students and others who may not fully understand or appreciate the splendid growth which has taken place at the Guelph Colleges over the past few years and the difficulties, financial and otherwise, which they might encounter if they were granted university status. I have come to the conclusion that, from the standpoint of the staff, the principal bone of contention is the loss of prestige to the colleges in not being able to grant their own degrees. I believe that if this situation could be corrected, the enthusiasm of the staff could very well be reflected to the student body. As well, such a move would be a definite and clear indication that the Bill to federate the Colleges at the last session was not just window dressing.[41]

The deputy minister's views did not prevail. No amendments were proposed to the act that continued in force until it was superseded by the creation of the University of Guelph. The Federated Colleges Act, and the companion legislation establishing an Agricultural Research Institute, were the last changes the Department of Agriculture introduced to the colleges at Guelph. The next change, creating a university, removed them altogether from the control of the department.

In the fall of 1962, no one in the Department of Agriculture or among the administrators of the Guelph colleges thought that university status was imminent. The common feeling was that the likelihood had receded for the moment and the task was now to make federation work. Within a few months, however, the idea of university status for Guelph had sprung up once again, this time at Queen's Park. The source was surprising. Leslie Frost, who as premier had found ways to stifle every proposal to create a university at Guelph, was a member of the re-constituted Advisory Committee on University Affairs and he decided early in 1963 that a university should be built at Guelph. His conversion was a vital prerequisite to the decision by the Robarts government to proceed. The change was sudden and unexpected. Now it was the Ontario government that virtually imposed a university on Guelph, sweeping aside the federation, which hardly had time to get started. When J.D. MacLachlan suggested a federation in 1961, following the defeat of his university proposal, he had no idea that a university would follow so rapidly, nor was he planning for this a year later. For the people at Guelph the premier's announcement, early in 1963, could not have been more startling.

The limestone house, known as the President's Residence, was built in 1882 for the professor of agriculture. Several OAC presidents occupied the house in this century. J.D. MacLachlan and his family lived there when he was president of OAC, then of the Federated Colleges and later still when he was president of the University of Guelph.

CHAPTER 4

Creating a University

The educational climate in Ontario underwent a very rapid transformation in the early 1960s. This was not a post-Sputnik reaction, a sense that higher education in the province had to be revolutionized if Canada was to catch up to the Russians in scientific advances. Indeed, there is little evidence that Canadian educational planners were really influenced by the Sputnik era debates that preoccupied the United States. The key element in the transformation was a belated realization of the magnitude of the enrolment crisis that would shortly wash over Ontario's universities like a tidal wave as the post-war baby boom generation reached university age. Population growth, not politics or economics, was the real reason for the reshaping of Ontario's system of higher education during the 1960s.[1]

As late as 1959 or 1960, Ontario politicians, including Leslie Frost, the premier, had not yet awakened to the full extent of the impending demographic shock. But within two years a new study prepared by Dr. Robert Jackson of the Department of Educational Research at the University of Toronto made both the academics of the province and government officials sit up and take notice. He surveyed both secondary school enrolment and university enrolment in the province and projected the likely university enrolment to 1971-2.

In 1960, Ontario had 32,000 full time students enrolled in its universities. In studies during the next two years, Jackson forecast this number would climb to 55,000 by 1965 and a minimum of 91,000 by 1970.[2] His figures, which had the impact of an earthquake on educators in 1962, proved in the end to be too conservative. In 1970 there were, in fact, 120,000 students in the province's university system. Until Jackson produced his statistical projections, Ontario government officials complacently believed a modest expansion of facilities would be able to cope with the influx. But they had seriously underestimated both the effect of the high immigration of the 1950s to Ontario and the rapidly growing participation rate as a steadily increasing percentage of the 18- to 24-year-old age group expressed its wish, if not its right, to attend university.

Jackson knew his figures would startle the educational and political establishment of the province. He saw his role as a gadfly, prodding and irritating especially the academic leaders to take some belated action to meet the looming crisis. Time was very short. Jackson described the reaction to his report in a letter to the senior civil servant in the Ministry of Education, F.S. Rivers, its chief director:

> My feeling is that they were for the first time shocked out of their complacency and really challenged to do something about the future. I think I know enough about my colleagues to promise you that now that they have been shocked out of their slumber in the upper levels of the ivory tower, they will get down to brass tacks and produce something in terms of plans and proposals.[3]

Jackson promised he would not let up in his constant pressure for action "in order to make sure that they do not relapse into a long slumber which would carry us into a critical period beyond which there would be no return." He did not have to worry about a relapse. His report accomplished what he desired. The creaky machinery of higher education in Ontario slowly began to chug into action to prepare plans to accommodate a hitherto unheard of number of new students.

Even before he became premier, John Robarts had been aware of the imminent challenges in higher education confronting Ontario. As minister of education in 1961, he had restructured the Advisory Committee on University Affairs, and when he replaced Leslie Frost as premier later that same year, he asked Frost to sit on the Advisory Committee, which was to study all aspects of the "establishment, development, operation, expansion and financing of universities in Ontario."[4] Robarts reiterated the government's aims for the committee when he met with its members at the end of June, 1961. The committee was to provide the government with a breadth of view on higher education in the province. Its very existence was meant to ensure that universities maintained their identity as independent institutions and to avoid any possibility of universities coming under government control. Above all, it was meant to co-ordinate university development in the province, a major task in view of the enrolment forecasts for the 1960s.[5] One analyst described the committee's mandate: "It was to be an adviser, a scrutineer, and a planner."[6] The committee, with former Premier Frost a vigorous member, played a crucial role in the expansion of Ontario's university system in the early 1960s.

When the committee received Robert Jackson's enrolment projections in the spring of 1962, it immediately commissioned the presidents of the Ontario universities to prepare a plan, outlining what measures should be adopted to meet the huge increase in enrolment. The presidents responded quickly with what became known as the Deutsch report, named after John Deutsch, later principal of Queen's University. The report was based on Jackson's projections, which the presidents had no trouble accepting as "the most reasonable minimum on which to base any analysis and prediction."[7]

According to the presidents, the government had very little time to act, since "the first shockwave of students" was expected in 1965 and 1966. "There may well be as many *freshmen* in 1966 as there are students today. In other words we face an unremitting expansion, of spasmodic intensity, with no contraction for the foreseeable future, and with major crises just three and four years ahead."[8] These were emotional words to describe what lay ahead, but they succeeded in paving the way for the adoption of the major elements in the report.

The Deutsch report, among other remedies, called for the creation of several three-year liberal arts colleges, each of them to be tied to an existing university that would grant degrees. Two would be located in Toronto and affiliated with the University of Toronto. One would be placed in Welland or St. Catharines and linked to McMaster, and one would be located in Peterborough and affiliated with Queen's. The government's decision to create Brock University in St. Catharines, Trent in Peterborough and two satellite campuses of the University of Toronto at Scarborough and Erindale evolved naturally from this recommendation. The Deutsch report was a utilitarian and practical document designed to "ensure the best preparation to the largest number of young people with the least expenditure of public funds and the greatest assurance of the maintenance of academic standards ..."[9]

Hidden in the body of the Deutsch report was a suggestion to consider starting arts courses at OAC by 1965. This was not, however, one of the official recommendations and it was not included in the summary of recommendations at the end of the report. With the prospect of two new satellite campuses, the University of Toronto was not anxious to assume the burden for a third one in Guelph. It was not at all clear from the Deutsch report or from the immediate reaction to it among members of the Advisory Committee on

University Affairs whether Guelph was to be included or left out. What was plain was that the government now desperately needed relatively cheap solutions to its higher education dilemma. Guelph offered the cheapest alternative in the province since many of the facilities were already in place. From 1962 on, provincial fiscal imperatives rather than OAC ambitions determined the fate of the Guelph campus.

There were other pressures weighing on the Advisory Committee on University Affairs. The prospect of having a university was irresistible to many Ontario communities. By July 1962, the Advisory Committee had a lengthy list of suitors: Chatham, Belleville, Sault Ste. Marie, Barrie, Oakville, Oshawa and Burlington, apart from those cities where approval had already been given.[10] Guelph was a significant omission. The city had made no official representations to obtain a university.

Some in the province, especially officials connected with the University of Toronto, worried about an unrestricted proliferation of universities that would dilute government funding and undermine standards. When the Advisory Committee met with the University of Toronto in December, 1962, Colonel E.P. Phillips, chairman of the University of Toronto Board of Governors, urged the government to make an unequivocal statement of its policy on higher education. "So long as that policy remains vague, the Government will continue to be increasingly badgered by local groups."[11] The University of Toronto believed that no new universities would be required until the 1970s and any new colleges should be affiliated with existing universities. The Toronto administration was willing to concede full university status to York, Assumption (Windsor), Laurentian, Waterloo and Carleton but only when they achieved "a greater degree of maturity in their own development."[12] What Toronto really wanted was to freeze the first stage of expansion where it was to prevent any further proliferation. None of the Guelph institutions was mentioned in this discussion even though the University of Toronto granted all Guelph degrees.

The suggestion in the Deutsch report of starting arts courses at Guelph was the only hint in official documents of what lay in store for the colleges. It did not even rank as an official recommendation for action by the Advisory Committee on University Affairs. Leslie Frost, however, did not require formal recommendations. He was used to acting on his own finely honed political instincts.

He had used the opportunity of public hearings earlier in 1962 to explore the future of OAC with the presidents of both the University of Western Ontario and Waterloo. Edward Hall, who had served as president of Western since 1947, was an OAC alumnus.

When Frost quizzed him about the future of OAC, Hall criticized the college "for moving away from being a good Agricultural college." He was also unhappy that OAC students were "getting the greatest subsidy of any students in Ontario."[13] President Hagey of Waterloo, responding to a query from Leslie Frost on the prospects for a partial integration of the facilities of Waterloo and Guelph, specified the practical obstacles that stood in the way, notably the timetabling of classes, and the lack of suitable transportation. These preliminary investigations into alternative solutions for Guelph proved abortive.

A year later, following the committee's receipt of both Jackson's report on future enrolment and the Deutsch report, Frost decided the time had come to find a solution for Guelph. He had long been convinced of the need to utilize the facilities at Guelph more efficiently. He told the Committee on University Affairs that there "ought to be a group of citizens in Guelph who would come together to establish a university and take over the responsibilities."[14] Part of his desire to find a local group of citizens to take over the colleges arose from his annoyance at what he believed to be occurring at Guelph. The OAC, according to Frost, had spread "into other fields which aren't agriculture," but the Department of Agriculture bore the expenses.[15] Frost still spoke as a former treasurer of the province. He could not eliminate the suspicions he had long harboured of the way money was spent at these government institutions. Turning responsibility over to an independent board of governors might be a way of bringing fiscal responsibility to OAC, as well as a cheap way of finding another university for the province.

The committee agreed with Frost that the province should create a university, which he suggested calling The University of Wellington. OAC would be affiliated with the new institution. Frost said he would discuss the proposal with cabinet members and mused, "We could take a gigantic step."[16] For the Guelph colleges it would indeed be a gigantic step, especially since it would come as a surprise announcement from Toronto without any advance notice or consultation.

Within two months, Leslie Frost had convinced John Robarts to proceed with the creation of a university at Guelph. Robarts himself made the announcement in the Ontario Legislature on February 27, 1963 on the occasion of the introduction of the estimates for the Department of Agriculture.

Robarts placed the Advisory Committee on University Affairs in charge of raising the three Guelph colleges to university status. In effect, this meant that Leslie Frost, who had for so many years blocked university status for Guelph, would ultimately be responsible for bringing it to fruition. Robarts announced that Guelph was to be "a full university" with each of the colleges as integral components. He was very careful at the same time to placate the agricultural community by stressing again how vital the colleges were for the province's agriculture. They existed, as they always had, to serve the needs of Ontario agriculture. This would not change. Robarts underlined how this "historic and very necessary function ... will be in no way impaired by this development but will, in my plans, be strengthened."[17]

Robarts accepted Frost's advice on the need for a citizens' committee to develop the university at Guelph "in the same way that we have developed our other universities throughout the province."[18] His announcement said the government would create one immediately. As a prospective university community, Guelph was unique in the province in not already having such a committee. The government viewed it primarily as a vehicle for fundraising. The governments of Frost and Robarts were opposed to the philosophy that all the funds to support universities should come from government. New universities should be located only where the community had demonstrated through successful fundraising that it was willing to bear a portion of the cost. This had not happened in Guelph, but the government was determined to apply the same model there.

Because of the importance of fundraising, businessmen played a key role in the creation of Ontario's new universities—Waterloo, York, Brock and Trent—primarily by raising funds to help the institutions begin operations and thus proving their viability to government.[19] Guelph would continue to be an exception to this pattern since no fund-raising campaign was launched until well after the university was in place. Businessmen did not create the university at Guelph even though local businessmen were involved in the process. Unlike all the other new universities that came into existence in this period, Guelph was an offspring of the state, despite government efforts to make it conform to what was seen as the acceptable norm.

The nucleus of a citizens' committee in Guelph appeared, however, even before the premier made his announcement in the Legislature. The initiative came from the chairman of the Board of Education in Guelph, a businessman named Tom McEwan. He was also a member of the Guelph Rotary Club and he recalls often asking Jim Schroder, a faculty member at OVC, why there was no university in Guelph. "We had all those buildings and that tremendous staff ... it appeared to me to be a place where we could expand university education rather quickly."[20] Schroder, in turn, challenged McEwan to do something and following a late night Board of Education meeting in November, 1962, McEwan initiated a discussion with several of his board colleagues. "I thought that the colleges on the hill would be a great place — a good foundation — for a university. I knew that Trent and Brock had started from nothing, just vacant land, and I felt that the colleges would not have to go through that 'starting from scratch' with all the assets they had up there."[21]

McEwan and two other Board of Education members, Aubrey Hagar and Gordon Tiller, proceeded then to organize a Guelph Citizens' Committee. This included some faculty members from the colleges such as Jim Schroder and Cliff Barker from OVC and Bill Brown from the Chemistry Department, which was then part of OAC. They did not want to be publicly identified because of their civil service status. The members of the Citizens' Committee were well aware of previous attempts to launch a campaign for university status. Their optimism stemmed from a realization of the enormous demand for university places, but they were realists. With a thriving University of Waterloo next door, a strong case was required and they knew they would have to overcome the fears of the agricultural community as well as those faculty members who still opposed the idea.[22]

Hagar was an OAC graduate and McEwan's successor as chairman of the Guelph school board. Later, he served as vice-president of Conestoga Community College. He recalled his own motives for participating:

> My personal philosophy was that students in agriculture, home economics and veterinary medicine were really being denied the presence of an arts faculty and I felt that the academic program was much too insular. You see the Colleges, in my view, lacked a vision or notions of what a more complete education was all about. In many respects, I think OAC and Macdonald Institute in particular and, in part, OVC, at that time were more technological institutions than colleges of a university and it seemed to me that for the very vitality of learning, a more broadly based program was necessary.[23]

At the time the Citizens' Committee was created, two faculty associations existed, one for OVC and one for OAC. The Citizens' Committee approached both associations for assistance in discovering faculty attitudes towards the possibility of a university. Together they conducted an informal poll that revealed a majority of about four to one in favour of university status. The Citizens' Committee also estimated the three colleges had the facilities to accept 1,000 more students without additional buildings, and in this way make a significant contribution in the looming crisis when the post-war baby boom reached university age.[24]

Tom McEwan recalls that when the Citizens' Committee began its work, he "could not find any open, or active, support for a university by any group or individual on campus. What existed was passive, frozen into silence."[25] On the committee's behalf, McEwan wrote to J.D. MacLachlan, president of the Federated Colleges, in early December, 1962, outlining the virtues of a university in Guelph and promising the co-operation of local industrialists, businessmen and educators in the campaign to obtain a university.[26] McEwan wanted MacLachlan and the Board of Regents to assume the leadership of the proposed campaign and to define a role for the Citizens' Committee. He assured MacLachlan that the Guelph newspapers and radio had pledged support. All that was needed was a signal from the authorities in the colleges themselves and the campaign could begin.

Part of McEwan's letter set out the "excellent qualifications" of the citizens of Guelph to have a university. "Among our citizens we have a relatively high proportion with university training. A greater percentage of our students proceed toward university entrance qualifications than is the case in most other centres in Ontario."[27] McEwan stressed that his colleagues on the Guelph Board of Education were "with one exception composed of college graduates." These points, combined with the fact that the three colleges "now have all the attributes of a first rate university," in McEwan's opinion, constituted a strong case for Guelph's aspirations.

MacLachlan took McEwan's letter to the Board of Regents of the Federated Colleges. Replying to McEwan, MacLachlan made it clear that neither he nor the board had any interest in a formal alliance with the Citizens' Committee. MacLachlan suggested that the committee approach Premier Robarts directly, but he made no overtures either for co-operation or assistance.[28]

The Citizens' Committee was affronted by such a negative reaction from the Board of Regents, but MacLachlan softened the blow by meeting privately with the organizers and encouraging them to proceed. Hagar remembered the meeting and how he had been "most impressed by Dr. MacLachlan's encouragement and counsel to us. Perhaps we would have pressed on anyway — such is the brashness of local politicians."[29]

The committee decided to forge ahead on its own and met on several occasions in the board room of the Cutten Golf Club, just across the road from the colleges. Two representatives of the OAC Faculty Association, E.V. (Ted) Evans and Gerry Trent, joined two representatives of the OVC Faculty Association, John Gilman and Don Barnum, so that the Citizens' Committee had the benefit of faculty advice. Don Barnum recalls that the Faculty Association representatives "prepared for the committee a plan for a university indicating the strength of the various departments and how facilities could be developed from them. It was an exciting exercise."[30] This was done without any knowledge of the views of the administration of the colleges or of the Department of Agriculture. One of the long-term benefits was to amalgamate the two college faculty associations to make possible the later direct action of the Federated Colleges Faculty Association. Macdonald Institute did not have a separate faculty association and neither of the other two associations felt an obligation to involve these predominantly female faculty members. John Gilman remembered this omission. "It was a reflection of that era that we were able to get away without consulting Macdonald Institute."[31]

The meetings of the Citizens' Committee focused on possible obstacles ranging from the administration of the Department of Agriculture to the political complexities and reaction of the people of Guelph. Hagar, who served as the committee's secretary, distilled the conclusions into a discussion paper entitled, "The Need for Increased University Facilities and the Federated Colleges," which the committee adopted as the basis of a brief to the Ontario government.[32] Hagar identified the critical lack of facilities for university education in the province at a time when the demand for university education was about to double or treble. He contrasted the solution already evident in the creation of infant universities requiring *"very large expenditures* for qualified faculty and staff, and the physical plant and equipment essential to higher education" with the much less expensive alternative of expanding *"existing institutions of moderate size."* Raising the federated colleges to university status, he speculated, could be accomplished with a very small increase in capital and operating costs. Hagar also stressed the value of permitting the colleges to offer postgraduate degrees, opening up new possibilities for programs especially in agriculture and veterinary science.

Hagar's paper directly confronted the old bogey about the potential damage to Ontario agriculture if the colleges received university status. "Such a dismal conclusion is by no means necessary."[33] He pointed out that the land grant universities in the United States were "doing a better job of serving agriculture than ever before." Within a university the agriculture departments could draw on a much wider range of support from other academic departments. The land grant universities also had been able to create agricultural experimental stations where specialized agricultural research could be carried out.

Early in 1963, the Citizens' Committee was finalizing arguments to be presented to the premier. Hagar summarized in a series of suggestions the advantages the committee foresaw. They included cultural, educational and financial benefits for the community of

Guelph, an increase in available resources for Ontario's rural community, a broadening of the educational experience of agriculture students, placing agricultural education "on a par" with other postsecondary education, more efficient use of the facilities already in place and a reduction in the cost per student.[34]

After further discussions, McEwan wrote to Premier Robarts on behalf of the Citizens' Committee on February 11, 1963.[35] The letter summarized the conclusions of the Citizens' Committee, making the case that the "Federated Colleges, adjacent to our City, seem to be most logical for a university programme." The chief argument was the utilitarian one. "Our studies strongly indicate no comparative situation exists in Ontario to expand university enrolment and maintain high standards at such relatively low cost."[36] What probably appealed most to the premier, however, was McEwan's optimism about the ability of the committee to raise funds. McEwan emphasized the non-partisan nature of the committee and its readiness to act as soon as the premier gave the signal. The committee also made sure that MacLachlan received a copy of the letter. Through MacLachlan it was on the desk of both the deputy minister of agriculture and W.A. Stewart, the minister, shortly after the premier received it.[37] The premier's response "that the future of OAC is being given very close scrutiny" was heartening and the speed with which the government acted surprised all the members of the committee.[38]

When Premier Robarts announced university status for the Federated Colleges on February 27, the Citizens' Committee naturally assumed its representation had been responsible. Some, at least, thought the work of the committee was finished. What none of them knew was that the government had made its initial decision without even knowing of the committee's existence. McEwan's letter enabled the premier to make it appear to the rest of the province that at Guelph the same model of local business support would be followed. Aubrey Hagar remembers the events of the spring of 1963 as "somewhat confusing." So they were. When the announcement was made in February, none of the groundwork had been prepared.[39] It was left ostensibly to the Committee on University Affairs, and especially to Leslie Frost, to implement what the premier had decreed.

The public reaction to the announcement of Premier Robarts was very positive. Within the Legislature, the opposition Liberals and NDP members welcomed what they saw as a long overdue change.[40] *The Globe and Mail's* education correspondent, J. Bascom St. John, was fulsome in his praise. He glowingly reviewed the history of OAC and its sister institutions, saying the money put into them was "one of the most fabulous investments the Government has ever made. Only the Hydro might possibly compare with the return in increased wealth produced." Adding an arts and science faculty to the nucleus of the Federated Colleges "is an obvious improvement and should have been done years ago." He looked ahead to "a university of immense dynamic which will set a fine pace for others."[41]

In Guelph itself, the *Daily Mercury*'s columnist, Verne McIlwraith, was more cautious, welcoming the prospect but adding that the same idea had been current for nearly twenty-five years. Since the premier himself announced it, McIlwraith said, "it seems to hold some measure of assurance that it will happen."[42]

The student paper, *The Ontarion*, revealed the inner tensions that would cause some strain as the university came into being. One editorial liked the idea of adding more arts courses "into our present highly science-concentrated curriculum ... At present we are unable to study Canadian literature."[43] A companion editorial supported "academic freedom and full-scale accreditation in the form of university status" but prophesied that a plan to build a complete arts faculty in Guelph "cannot but lead to a partial submergence of the traditional function of OA-VC-Mac."[44]

Behind the public praise there was confusion among the politicians and civil servants at Queen's Park over what to do next. The Committee on University Affairs held a long discussion of the Guelph issue when it met on March 28, 1963. The letter from Robarts to the Guelph Citizens' Committee was read and the Advisory Committee then deliberated at great length over the appropriate composition of the committee. An air of unreality hung over the discussion. Leslie Frost talked eagerly of reorganizing the Guelph committee under the chairmanship of his former cabinet minister from Guelph, Bill Hamilton, a "highly respectable fellow," as if the task was a local election.[45] Certainly Frost's enthusiasm for plunging in and reorganizing the group at Guelph was akin to that of the old political warhorse anxious to fight another campaign. Under Frost's guidance, the Advisory Committee on University Affairs wanted to have the Guelph Citizens' Committee more broadly representative of the community than the one that had come forward. As soon as Bill Hamilton had carried out the necessary consultations, Leslie Frost's University Advisory Committee would visit Guelph and meet with the revamped committee.[46] There was apparently no thought or suggestion of meeting with the president of the Federated Colleges or the Board of Regents to plan the next step. J.D. MacLachlan knew no more about the government's intentions than anyone else and he certainly was not told by Leslie Frost or any of his colleagues on the Advisory Committee on University Affairs.

In Guelph, the Citizens' Committee under T.A. McEwan was busy assembling a list of suitable names that was sent to the premier.

At the same time, Bill Hamilton, who had been contacted by Leslie Frost, approached the city council and asked them to form a citizens' committee. Council duly obliged and sent a list to the Board of Regents of the Federated Colleges.[47] With each of the participants sending lists of names to the others, the momentum for a citizens' committee to launch the new university began to dissipate. Anger and cynicism replaced the initial mood of almost euphoric optimism.

The Board of Regents had never endorsed the Citizens' Committee and had no intention of yielding its powers prematurely. Fred Presant, the veteran OAC alumnus who chaired the board, wrote to the Guelph City Council stating that "the concept of establishing a Citizens' Committee was initiated independent of the Colleges, and of the Board, and there is reason to think this approach should be maintained until the composition of the Citizens' Committee is finally endorsed by either the Prime Minister or the University Affairs Committee."[48] When Tom McEwan, the chairman of the original Citizens' Committee, read Presant's letter, he was angry and decided to be very blunt in a letter to Premier Robarts. McEwan informed the premier "that progress towards a University in Guelph has stopped and confusion and disillusionment is setting in …. Leadership and positive action which is clearly understood as steps towards University status, is becoming more critical each day the situation drifts."[49] McEwan wanted Robarts to act before more damage was done.

Leslie Frost, too, was frustrated at the lack of progress in Guelph when the Advisory Committee on University Affairs next met in Kingston in May. He had a different explanation, reflecting his traditional ambivalence towards the colleges. In Frost's eyes they wanted to be a university "and engage in everything in a farmer's college." There were more people there from Toronto because the fees and board were low. "It's the highest cost institution in Ontario." He also hit out at the people in Guelph who were "not the ambitious [types] that they have in Peterborough because Government is picking up the tab."[50] Frost was dissuaded from going to Guelph to organize them himself, but clearly the hopes for a citizens' committee to create a university were foundering.

The confusion about the role of a citizens' committee in creating the university was matched by the uncertainty both in Guelph and at Queen's Park over the exact nature of the university that had been announced. Would the Federated Colleges be a part of it or would they continue to exist as a separate entity supported by the Department of Agriculture? What new faculties would be required? How would the university be governed and financed? These and other questions had to be addressed with haste because no plans had been approved by the government before the premier's announcement in February, 1963.

J.D. MacLachlan, president of the Federated Colleges, had been working on his own plan for a university since 1957. He happily set to work again in March, 1963, now that he could see his long desired goal as a real possibility at last. When the Board of Regents of the Federated Colleges met in March, 1963, it requested MacLachlan to prepare an appraisal of the campus for university development.[51] He completed his assessment before the end of March and sent it to the deputy minister of agriculture for the use of the Advisory Committee on University Affairs.[52]

His brief pointed out that except for what he termed "technicalities," the Guelph campus was already functioning as a university. With only 700 residence beds, there was an obvious shortage of accommodation for additional students, most of whom would come from outside Guelph. Most important, however, for MacLachlan and his colleagues in the Federated Colleges, was the character this new university would assume. He underlined in this document, as he had in all his earlier submissions, that the "continuation of identity with rural Ontario should be an objective of the university."

The key addition, as he recognized, would be an arts and science college "as a companion to the three Colleges now on campus." Accommodating those students seeking higher education in the arts and sciences was, after all, the primary motive for the government's decision to transform the Guelph campus into a university. But this transformation could not occur without new facilities and faculty. MacLachlan argued against commencing undergraduate programs in the arts until the appropriate faculty and facilities were in place. A new library and a building to accommodate the humanities and social sciences were minimum requirements.

MacLachlan well knew that the size of the university would profoundly affect its character. To protect the role of the federated colleges and their students, he was anxious to prevent the university from growing too large, for in a large university the arts and science students might overwhelm the others. Retaining the traditions of the campus was a governing element in his recommendation for a campus of 5,000 to 6,000 students, half to two-thirds of them in arts or science programs. He argued the case for graduate programs in agriculture and veterinary medicine and pictured the advantages for agricultural research stemming from a university campus.

MacLachlan's brief was a very practical, down-to-earth document, befitting its author. He did not sketch a visionary future or a radical approach for the new institution. His one tentative step towards innovation was a comment on society's need for students with ability in languages. As he observed, the language barriers to communication among people of the world needed to be overcome.

> Whether it be the teaching of French and other languages in our schools or the preparation of university graduates to effectively participate in affairs stretching from Ontario to various parts of the world, there is an apparent dearth in the number of those sufficiently versatile in even the major languages and in the history and culture of the countries involved.[53]

MacLachlan also presented his brief to the Board of Regents of the Federated Colleges at the June meeting when the board unanimously approved it as a working document to develop the academic basis of the university.[54] The board also authorized MacLachlan, along with the deans of OAC and OVC and the director of the Agricultural Research Institute, to visit Cornell during the summer. MacLachlan then went to the Universities of Arizona and California to see what could be learned in planning a university. During the 1950s, when discussions about the future direction of OAC occurred, Britain and Europe had been the places to visit. Now the United States experience was to guide the academic administrators of the Federated Colleges.

Their visit to Cornell in July convinced the heads of the Guelph colleges to make their university emulate Cornell as closely as possible. The ideal solution would be to create an Ontario Cornell at Guelph. This conviction arose from the shared desire to strengthen what they saw as the historic functions of the three existing colleges so they could flourish within a larger university framework. Cornell administered four state colleges for the State University of New York — an agricultural college, a college of home economics, a veterinary school and a school of industrial and labour relations. Could a university at Guelph be structured similarly?

Dean N.R. Richards of OAC was impressed by the autonomy of the Board of Governors at Cornell and he believed the Cornell model had the answers to the challenges Guelph faced. His objective for the new university to provide greater service to agriculture and rural Ontario could best be met by importing Cornell's structure. Dean Trevor Lloyd Jones of OVC agreed. He wanted to scrap the Federated Colleges, which he had never liked, and replace them with a university governed by an autonomous Board of Governors. Dean Jones concluded his report after visiting Cornell with a burst of optimism about the future of Guelph:

I feel sure that we need a vital and even daring approach to the development of "our" university. If the charter delegates responsibility and power to responsible citizens, with freedom to do almost anything that is consistent with making higher education available to anyone who is of a calibre to accept it, I think we could be the forerunners of a new era so far as university education is concerned in this country. Expansion in adult education is just one of several fields that would suit our tradition; the encouragement of rural people to become interested in new vistas, is another.[55]

The visit to Cornell had an equally profound effect on J.D. MacLachlan. On his return from his study of the American universities, he prepared a revised plan for the Guelph university, explicitly based on the Cornell model. He sent this in August to the deputy minister of agriculture for the Advisory Committee on University Affairs to use.[56] He also sent a second brief, assessing the various alternatives.[57] His design recognized and provided for sufficient resources to enable the existing colleges to maintain their current and anticipated functions "in the agricultural pattern." This was why, of the four options he presented, MacLachlan rejected all but the Cornell idea. He explicitly excluded the concepts of a university at Guelph "on the same basis as the other Ontario universities," a state-supported land grant type of university, and a new university solely for arts and sciences to which the federated colleges would be affiliated.

A university created on the same lines as the rest in the province might precipitate a reaction from the agricultural community because of the potential loss of identity for agriculture and, he argued, a board of governors could not find the necessary resources itself to finance all the agricultural research and allied services. "Such a concept would be comparable to asking the governing board of Carleton University to be responsible for the maintenance of the Central Experimental Farm." A state-supported land grant type of university would arouse opposition from all the other Ontario universities, and most likely from the University of Toronto whose act designated it as the provincial university of Ontario. Affiliating the existing Federated Colleges to a new university would create problems of internal efficiency, conflicts of interest and dual allegiance on the part of faculty, students and staff.

Having rejected the three other possibilities, MacLachlan extolled the virtues of the Cornell model where an independent board of governors controlled all the faculties of the university, but operated the professional faculties on a contract from the government. MacLachlan foresaw that by using this model, many features created in the Federated Colleges could be retained. The new university would, in fact, have two sections under the control of a single board of governors. One would be the three Department of Agriculture colleges and the other would consist of two university colleges, one for graduate studies and one for undergraduate arts and sciences.

The university colleges would be financed for operating and capital purposes in the same way as other Ontario universities, but the Department of Agriculture colleges would receive operating funds through a contract between the university and the Department of Agriculture and all their buildings would be financed and run by the Department of Public Works. MacLachlan saw a number of advantages in this hybrid Cornell model for a university. The public identity of the existing colleges would be retained, the connection with the Department of Agriculture would not be lost and a centralized administration for all the colleges would mean greater efficiency.

MacLachlan also visited the University of California campus at Davis before he prepared his master plan. There he learned an important lesson, one he was quick to pass on both to the Ontario government and to his own Board of Regents. When he listened to the history of the development of the California Davis campus, MacLachlan remarked on the similarity to the Guelph experience. At Davis, agriculture came first and was predominant. MacLachlan learned that in 1951 when the College of Letters and Science was introduced, the agricultural public expressed fears that their beloved "friendly farmers'" campus would be submerged. To counteract these fears, the College of Letters and Science was established "as a relatively minor and subservient entity."[58] This decision, MacLachlan discovered, was later universally acknowledged as an error that the administrators at Davis were left to rectify. As MacLachlan wrote,

> Wherever I went, and to whomever I talked, whether senior administrators or faculty, I received the same concept. 'The strength and contribution of your professional colleges is contingent to a large extent upon the strength of your colleges in arts and sciences.'[59]

MacLachlan returned from Davis with one other piece of advice ringing in his ears. Develop a documented campus plan as the first step in developing your university, he was told, and it will help to avoid expensive errors.

These precepts remained with MacLachlan and became part of the educational philosophy as he presided over the transition of the Guelph campus. His carefully worked out organizational plan for an Ontario Cornell, however, joined all his previous attempts at designing university structures for Guelph as archival relics. Although officials in the Departments of Agriculture and Education and members of the premier's Advisory Committee on University Affairs carefully read MacLachlan's brief and Robarts and his ministers of education and agriculture all examined it, in the end the government decided against the Cornell model. Innovations were risky and might well offend other universities across the province especially if Guelph were seen to receive favoured treatment in government funding. When the legislation appeared in 1964 to create the University of Guelph, it followed the pattern already set for Ontario's other new universities. Guelph would be unique in Ontario, but it would not be a carbon copy of Cornell. Again the explanation lay in events at Queen's Park.

Gordon Couling

The current Alumni House started its life as a carriage house, was converted to a sheep barn in the 1920s and was rebuilt in 1987. In 1982, the City of Guelph designated the exterior of the wooden structure as a historic site.

CHAPTER 5

The University of Guelph

Seven months after the announcement by Premier Robarts in the Legislature that a university would be built at Guelph, very little had happened to transform promise into reality. The Advisory Committee on University Affairs, with Leslie Frost as its acting chairman, had not met with either the Guelph Citizens' Committee or the Board of Regents of the Federated Colleges. The only meeting to occur over the summer of 1963 took place between Fred Presant, the chairman of the Board of Regents, and Leslie Frost. They agreed to defer all decisions about the nature of the university until after the September provincial election.[1]

With an election looming, some of the premier's supporters, including Minister of Agriculture William Stewart, worried about the political implications of an arts college at Guelph overshadowing or even obliterating the influence of the other three colleges. Stewart recalls warning Robarts and his other cabinet colleagues "that there was this danger and we'd better be sure we weren't doing something that we would later regret."[2] The issue did not surface during the campaign. Nor did Stewart change the premier's mind. "Robarts was absolutely adamant."[3] There would be a university at Guelph, and, as Stewart remembers, "The onus was kept on the uniqueness of the university." It would be the only one in Ontario, and one of a very few in the country, to include an agriculture college and a veterinary college.

The premier was intent on carrying out his commitment, but civil servants in the Departments of Agriculture and Education still could not agree on the nature of the university Guelph would become. In the Department of Agriculture, the prospect of having the three colleges absorbed into a larger university was worrisome to say the least. Great efforts were made to ensure lasting guarantees and genuine protection for the interests of the colleges. After digesting J.D. MacLachlan's proposed organizational plan, Deputy Minister Everett Biggs insisted the three colleges had to be fully integrated elements of the new university. "They would, through history, be recognized as founders and would continue to grow in relative stature within the university complex; on this basis, too, alumni would be motivated to support the new university."[4] If the colleges existed only as affiliates, or in Biggs's words, "segregated sisters of a growing giant," they would soon be overwhelmed. President Sydney Smith had used a cowbird metaphor in 1957 in speculating about the character of a university at Guelph. Everett Biggs found the metaphor helpful in 1963 to articulate his anxieties about the fate of the Federated Colleges as affiliates in a large arts and science university. To make the colleges affiliates, he believed, "might be considered analogous to the tactics of the cowbird which lays an egg in the established nest of another but potentially smaller breed. The mother bird, rightful owner of the nest, dutifully nourishes the cowbird fledgling along with her own but, because of growth rate to a much larger size, the former soon becomes the predominant occupant."[5] Biggs was determined to protect what he saw as the Department of Agriculture's own fledglings. His timetable for legislation contemplated a longer period of gradual change.

Legislation creating the university would be introduced in 1964. Two years later an amendment to the act would embody a College of arts and science and then, during the next three years, a gradual adjustment of the relations between the Federated Colleges, the Department of Agriculture and the university could take place. By phasing the change over six years, Biggs believed both the interests of the Department of Agriculture and those of the Federated Colleges would be better protected. This way the fledglings would have more time to adjust and the change would be less traumatic. In his proposal, Biggs also envisaged a continuing role for the Department of Agriculture in financing the teaching and research carried out in agriculture. Stewart took his deputy's recommendations, and MacLachlan's plan on which they were based, to Premier Robarts on October 18.[6]

Until 1963, the Department of Agriculture had the deciding voice in any change affecting the Guelph colleges. Now that the university issue was in the air, however, officials in the Department of Education put on the table some radically different alternatives of their own for Guelph. Even at this late date, the government of Premier Robarts had to make a choice between diametrically opposed blueprints of what the new university would be.

J.R. McCarthy, the secretary of the Advisory Committee on University Affairs and a superintendent of curriculum in the Ministry of Education — he would soon become the first deputy minister in the new Department of University Affairs — sketched out a vision for a state "University of Ontario" in several memoranda written in October, 1963.[7] His chief concern was how the province would accommodate the burgeoning university population. Where officials in the Department of Agriculture were looking for ways to insulate the colleges at Guelph from the impact of change, McCarthy saw an ideal opportunity at Guelph for the province to step in and provide innovative leadership with a state university. He pointed to the precedents of state universities in the United States and he warned that if there were further delays, Guelph would not be able to meet the rush for university places expected to begin in September, 1965. He had not detected any "great enthusiasm by local people to undertake the task" of organizing an independent Board of Governors at Guelph. Why couldn't the province go ahead and create a state university, which could be turned over to an independent Board of Governors later if that was thought desirable?

McCarthy itemized twelve advantages of a government-run university at Guelph. Because the nucleus of buildings, staff and equipment was already there, the OAC tradition would continue and extension into new disciplines would be easily facilitated. Government experimentation with special academic programs would be easier because all aspects, including evaluation, could be concentrated in one university. McCarthy was thinking not only of new courses or fields of study, but also of new teaching techniques including television. By using Guelph as a centre for experimentation in higher education, the province would avoid expensive duplication: "demonstrations of promising and successful experiments could be easily arranged and the results disseminated widely, and encouragement by example would be possible."[8] Concentrating experiments in one university would circumvent delays. "Besides, it could be ensured that novel approaches received sympathetic consideration and proper trial; universities are so conservative that many promising leads are either throttled at birth or an experiment with them is sabotaged from the outset."[9]

McCarthy foresaw that this state university could pioneer a standard "modest but adequate" design for residences and dormitories to ensure equal opportunity of access to university for students "from isolated areas of the province." It could also "provide a yardstick of costs and administration" to measure the efficiency of operation of other universities. New innovations like TV programs or other media could be made available "at reasonable cost" to the rest of the province. The university could establish a "mother college" to which community colleges or junior colleges could affiliate. Fields of study where there was a significant social need, as in professional training of elementary teachers, could be begun quickly at a state university.

McCarthy envisaged an enterprising pioneering state university setting an example for what he saw as the conservative, traditional private universities of the province. This concept no doubt arose partly from his frustration at the agonizing reluctance of the universities to act in the face of sudden and overwhelming enrolment pressures that had to be addressed by the government. McCarthy sensed this was only one element in a wider pattern of increasingly rapid social and technological evolution that he believed could only be addressed by a state university. "Only a state-operated university could adapt or be adapted in time to cope with the developing situation."

Although no one at the Federated Colleges ever had the opportunity to see McCarthy's radical dream for the campus, much less to assess it, he summed it up this way. "The OAC complex might truly become the 'University of Ontario' leaving the other institutions free to pursue their traditional endeavours." The government, too, he predicted, "would be in a much stronger position to influence university policies and practices, and without being forced to use one or more of the devices of bribery, blackmail, or threat of force. Leadership is essential, not uncontrolled competition or monopoly; probably this leadership can best be given, by precept and example, through the medium of a state university co-existing in a family of diverse types, but all welcomed as serving ultimately the same high purpose."[10]

McCarthy understood the universities of the province and foresaw how they would likely react to his proposal for a state university. He carefully outlined the arguments they might use. First was the expected criticism of one institution receiving one hundred per cent of its financial support direct from government when the others were forced to depend on private support for some of their resources. McCarthy dismissed this potential criticism on the grounds that the Federated Colleges had received all their financial support from government for a long time and had granted degrees through the University of Toronto. He was more concerned with actions he feared the other universities might take, either restricting their admissions to force the Ontario university to admit all the additional students, especially those with lower marks, or increasing their fees as a device to push more students to the Ontario university. McCarthy had answers for each of these possibilities. He would impose quotas for freshmen at all Ontario universities so that the burden would be shared equitably, and he would raise fees at the state university, but in combination with bursaries for rural students.

Underlying these hypothetical criticisms was a much larger philosophical issue that McCarthy outlined in considerable detail for William Davis, his minister of education, and for Premier Robarts. What role would be played by government in the higher education system of the province? The other Ontario universities would very likely view the creation of a state university at Guelph as "an infringement on the autonomy of university education ..."

McCarthy carefully described the key change that had occurred in the delicate relationship between universities and government. Universities had a jealously guarded tradition of independence from government that included financial independence. With the rapid expansion of postsecondary education during the previous decade — an expansion that would accelerate in the next decade — all universities in the province were becoming ever more dependent on government for revenue. McCarthy suggested that "in many respects, the universities then became a branch of government" even if they were not subject to the financial control or audit of government departments.

Growing financial dependence on government was one manifestation of the changed situation. Because of the vital importance of higher education to the welfare of the state, McCarthy argued that "the state has not only the right but the duty of determining that every field of study which is in the national interest is being pursued, that the number of graduates is adequate and that the resources are being used efficiently and economically." How the state resolved the relationship between universities and government was, for McCarthy, the fundamental question. His suggestion of sponsoring a state university was part of an experiment to find an answer because the government would then commit itself to fostering a variety of university types that would have to learn to function together.

He recognized as well that questions of academic freedom might be involved in the larger relationship of universities and government. McCarthy observed somewhat cynically "that the academics in Ontario fervently believe and loudly proclaim that scholarship, research and teaching flourish only under complete freedom. Experience at OAC and elsewhere would seem to cast doubt on the universality of this sentiment and on its validity, but the existence of this attitude must be recognized." McCarthy's answer here was that the existence of a variety of institutions would make it possible for an academic to move from one type to another if conditions at one proved impossible. He dismissed, however, the notion that academic freedom was less possible in a state university, while adding revealingly, "although irresponsible criticisms of government policy and practices would certainly be discouraged."[11]

McCarthy distilled his thoughts on the future of the Federated Colleges from five years' service as secretary to the Advisory Committee on University Affairs, which had discussed the transformation of the Guelph campus to a university as a regular part of its agenda. He had heard all the arguments and read all the documents. His solution was the most radical of any that had been advanced. Had it been adopted, the Ontario university system would have evolved very differently. McCarthy's memoranda were not made public. They went to the cabinet and presumably were read by Leslie Frost and his colleagues on the Advisory Committee.

Leslie Frost and his Advisory Committee met again at the end of October, 1963. Guelph took up a major portion of their agenda. Frost ruefully acknowledged that little had been accomplished since the premier's announcement the previous February. The committee then candidly assessed McCarthy's proposal. They knew they could recommend a state university, forcing the government to make the decision and accept the consequences, but there was very little enthusiasm for this initiative on the committee. One member pointed out that the idea ran contrary to the history of postsecondary education in the province. Another commented that a state university would set a standard for salaries across the province that would become the model for all other institutions. Frost expressed his own opinion with characteristic bluntness, "I think it would be impossible." He added that there was everything to lose and nothing to gain. For Leslie Frost, it was in the end a political decision and one the premier would have to make. If Robarts came down in favour of a state university, Frost would go along, but he did not believe the premier favoured the idea.[12] Neither did William Stewart, the minister of agriculture. He remembers how upset he was to hear the proposal.

> Well, I guess it was my Conservative background and rural background again coming to the fore. I was not very sympathetic to the idea simply because I felt it would upset the OAC and the OVC. I really did...I could just see the heather getting right on fire. I thought it was some far out academic idea and maybe I think I used that terminology or worse in discussing it with somebody down there, but it never really took off.[13]

McCarthy's plan for a state "Ontario University" at Guelph proved to be politically unacceptable, leaving the politicians and their advisers at the end of 1963 exactly where they had been at the beginning of the year, committed to the principle of a university at Guelph but still uncertain of its nature or composition. The student newspaper had published an open letter to the premier in October, facetiously suggesting new names for the proposed university. Two were "Political Football University" and "Hamlet University to be or not to be."[14] This student humour touched a raw nerve because it mirrored the political reality in the latter part of 1963.

Pressure was building on the Robarts government to announce its plans for the university at Guelph and to introduce legislation to establish the university. Other groups were now lobbying the government, trying to fashion the new institution in their interests. The Faculty Association of the Federated Colleges had not been consulted in any formal manner either by the academic heads of the colleges or by government officials prior to the Robarts announcement in February, 1963. Reacting to the lack of consultation, the association formed a university government committee and the brief it prepared went to the deputy minister of agriculture early in May, 1963. Faculty at the colleges decided they must be heard at Queen's Park.

> The colleges being a section of a government department are treated as such. We are informed about important changes in organization, in research and teaching policies, about new building programs, about new appointments etc. quite often only through newspapers or television. The opinion of the faculty as a whole on important matters is never really sought.[15]

The brief underscored the importance of founding the government of the proposed university on democratic principles. "After all, universities are looked on as being bastions of democracy and we should practise what we preach." This meant ensuring that the independent voice of faculty members could be heard and making decisions on academic policy matters after "careful research of all the facts, responsible debate and majority vote."[16] The Faculty Association had tried, without success, to gain direct representation on the Board of Regents and now the association prepared to campaign again to influence the composition of a university board of governors and more particularly the senate.

Before the Robarts government introduced the legislation for the University of Guelph, the Faculty Association of the Federated Colleges prepared a more extensive submission. Behind this was an eagerness to change the basis of university government, something faculty at the Guelph colleges shared with their colleagues across the country.

Professor Jim Stevens of the Physics Department attended the 1963 annual meeting of the Canadian Association of University Teachers at Laval as the delegate of the Federated Colleges Faculty Association. A year before, the National Conference of Canadian Universities and Colleges (now the AUCC) had endorsed a recommendation from CAUT to undertake a study of university government. What became the Duff-Berdahl Commission began in 1963 and, as Jim Stevens recalls, "the sense of 'Duff-Berdahl' was in the air."[17]

Stevens returned from the CAUT annual meeting "shocked at the differences between the governance of the Federated Colleges and the sense of 'what should be' as it was discussed at Laval. I'd been at Guelph for almost six years then and I remember returning home, and writing a report extolling the virtues of shared responsibility, collegial atmosphere, chairmen instead of heads, and limited-term administrative appointments instead of 'life' appointments. My report condemned the practices at Guelph and, I believe, fired up the Faculty Association executive."[18]

One of the leading members of the Faculty Association knew Angus Dunbar, a prominent Guelph lawyer who was also well connected in the Conservative party and a close friend of Leslie Frost. Through this connection, the Faculty Association was able to arrange a meeting at the end of January, 1964 with J.R. McCarthy in his capacity of secretary to the Advisory Committee on University Affairs and Everett Biggs, the deputy minister of agriculture.

The brief covered three points, all of great concern to the faculty in this transition period — the nature of university government, the transfer of the existing facilities and the protection of pensions. The first point continued their earlier submission and included a specific request for direct faculty representation on the board of governors. Their rationale eloquently spoke to the transcendent nature of the university in modern society:

> There is a very real danger that the multiplication of external pressures on universities and increases in size and complexity may interfere with and obscure the basic functions of the University, which must surely be the advancement of all areas of learning through teaching and research. Unfettered and continuous search for knowledge and truth in the humanities, the physical sciences and the social sciences is essential to the conservation and progress of a democratic system such as that enjoyed by the people of Ontario. This search can only be carried out in an environment protected from both the direct and overt influence of pressure groups whether political, industrial

or professional. Though seemingly paradoxical, it is none-theless true that the universities can best serve society if they are protected from it.[19]

For these faculty, the most secure protection would be a combination of faculty representation on the board of governors and "a strong form of democratic internal self government." Six of the eight principles appended to the brief described the self-government the faculty wanted: consultation between faculty, administration and the governing body on all major policy issues; a senate with a majority of elected faculty, the primacy of the senate in determining academic policy and plans for physical expansion; a board of governors to be a property holding body responsible for financial affairs and representing "the public conscience;" close collaboration between the senate and board; and due consultation with concerned faculty prior to making academic appointments.[20] The Faculty Association also asked to be consulted in the drafting of the university act.

Their remaining two principles called for the title of all property and capital facilities to be transferred to the university. The prospect of division between university and government over property ownership did not appeal to the faculty. They also rejected any form of dual ownership. This did not mean they were any the less dedicated to the special place of agriculture in the university. This was particularly recognized, but the brief concluded that "any dichotomy on the campus at Guelph would ... be detrimental to the best interests of the University and of Agriculture."[21]

The faculty members of the Federated Colleges were members of Ontario's civil service and enjoyed all the benefits of the civil service, including the civil service pension plan. For many of these faculty, the major obstacle and concern about a university at Guelph was the loss of these benefits. The association recognized the importance of pensions in its brief and asked for an equivalent pension plan to be implemented in the new university.

No specific promises were made to the Faculty Association representatives, but their views received an extensive hearing. The demand for direct faculty representation on the board of governors was ahead of its time. In 1963 it was not acceptable to a government trying to fashion legislation as similar as possible for the various new universities being created. Nor did the association achieve any dramatic new breakthroughs in creating a novel form of internal self-government for their proposed university. They had, however, articulated a viewpoint, based on their own Federated College experience, which shortly would be widely adopted across the country. Eventually most of their requests, including faculty representation on the board of governors, would be implemented at Guelph.

The initial Senate of the university, with its six faculty representatives chosen from the faculty at large, enshrined the principle of democratically elected faculty representatives. One of them was the chairman of the Faculty Association, John Gilman. He recalls attaining elected faculty on the Senate as "the major achievement of the Federated Colleges Faculty Association" in shaping the format of the new university.[22]

The faculty were not alone in visiting Queen's Park to make specific representations. Early in January of 1964, the Alumni Association of the Ontario Agricultural College arranged an appointment with William Stewart to express their concerns with the lack of progress in implementing the government's plans. They handed Stewart a brief urging prompt and decisive action. "We are convinced that to allow the situation to drift much longer can do irreparable harm to future development."[23] The alumni made one last attempt to revive the notion of a state university for their alma mater, proposing the name "University of Ontario" to put it on the same basis as the universities of Manitoba, Saskatchewan, Alberta, British Columbia and New Brunswick. It was not to be. Premier Robarts made the decision himself in January, 1964, and he named the institution to emphasize two things. It was to be a university like the others already established in the province and, regardless of the aspirations of alumni or others, it was not going to be a state university.

The Advisory Committee on University Affairs met on January 7, 1964, and Leslie Frost reported this decision to the committee members. He coloured his explanation with his own personal assessment. J.D. MacLachlan's ambition to retain the colleges and establish a university had been, in Frost's eyes, an obstacle. So was the attitude of the city and area that had been "spoon-fed for so long" with government funds and was looking for more. The solution would overcome these difficulties. The University of Guelph would be created as a "new creature" with J.D. MacLachlan in charge at the start. There would be no state university and, for the time being, the Federated Colleges would still retain their connection with the Department of Agriculture. Frost remained frustrated that his plans for a local group to run the university had not worked out, but he was now willing to have the government make the key decisions. "This is one place we're in position to dictate the terms." His last comment, "let the takeover of [the] farmer colleges come by evolution," did not reflect a desire to downplay the role of agriculture, but a realistic assessment that the days of the so-called farmers' colleges as government-run institutions had passed even if it would take some time to effect the change.[24]

Premier Robarts summoned J.D. MacLachlan to a meeting in Toronto on January 9, 1964, the first time the two men had actually met to discuss the proposed university. There was not a lot to discuss since Robarts had made the key decision. MacLachlan reiterated a point he had made all along that the Federated Colleges had to be fully integrated in the university, and he persuaded the premier to make a slight change in the proposed name. Robarts planned to name it "Guelph University" but MacLachlan persuaded him to change it to the "University of Guelph" to avoid nicknames like "Goo-U" or "Guru."[25] Nicknames could not be avoided, but the new name stuck.

When MacLachlan reported what had happened to his Board of Regents at the beginning of February, he was at a loss to explain the sequence of events. Very little had followed the Robarts outline of a year earlier. The Advisory Committee on University Affairs had never met with the Board of Regents, or with the Citizens' Committee, and MacLachlan's own carefully designed plans for the organization of the campus, intended for the Advisory Committee, had not been discussed with him at any meeting of the committee. Even the Board of Regents had not taken up the question of university status since the previous June. MacLachlan still did not know exactly how the government intended to structure the University of Guelph, and when he called the deans' councils of the three colleges together to brief them, he had nothing to present but "premises, presumptions, assumptions and wishful thinkings."[26] MacLachlan was the president-designate, but the provincial government was very much in charge.

Once the premier had decided to proceed, the pace of events picked up. The Speech from the Throne opening the legislative session at the beginning of 1964 included a commitment to introduce a bill to create the University of Guelph. This was most welcome news on the campus of the Federated Colleges. The editor of the student newspaper summed it up:

> The history of the last twenty-five years of these institutions has been one of frustration. Everything has been dependent upon whether or not we would become a university ...
>
> University status will also help bridge the gulf between those two large areas of learning—the arts and sciences. The greatest deficit in our present education is a lack of contact with arts students and the areas they deal with—abstract thought and ideas.[27]

Premier Robarts gave the task of preparing the legislation to the Department of Education. J.R. McCarthy drafted the bill, patterning it along the lines of the other new universities. It was ready in March and scheduled to be introduced in April. In an unusual gesture, Premier Robarts personally introduced it in the Legislature on April 24 for its first reading. Normally, the minister of education introduced legislation prepared by his department, but in this case the premier thought the minister of agriculture should do it. William Stewart recalls that he had to persuade the premier to introduce the legislation. Stewart believed that "it was an historic event and I also felt that it was so far-reaching it was far beyond the purview of the minister of agriculture. And I recall him saying to me, 'Well, if I have to introduce the bill, then you'll have to carry it through.'"[28]

Stewart was still worried about the potential political fallout in the agricultural community from the creation of the university. Having the premier make the announcement would help to defuse any latent concern. Robarts made sure that in his opening remarks he reiterated that "nothing ... either outlined in this bill or contemplated for the future, is intended to change the traditional role which has been filled by the federated colleges."[29] The government, Robarts claimed, looked forward to the strengthening of both the position and the programs of the existing colleges in the "truly new institution" being launched.

A section of the bill provided for the colleges to become part of the university, but for a period of time their association with the Department of Agriculture would continue. The premier did signal that "this relationship will, in time, change."[30] The rest of his speech outlined the government's need for more university spaces and Guelph's ability to provide some of these. Just how many turned out to be an additional shock for J.D. MacLachlan, publicly named president of the university by the premier, who did not choose to let a new Board of Governors make the choice. MacLachlan was in the balcony listening to the speech when Robarts speculated that Guelph might reach a student population of 15,000 by 1980. The new president "shuddered."[31] MacLachlan had always wanted to keep Guelph small enough so that the agriculture students would not be swamped and the intimacy of a smaller university would not disappear. He felt that officials in the Department of Education had become overexcited by the pressure to find university places and convinced the premier to plan a university at Guelph larger than it needed to be.[32]

Also in the audience was T.A. McEwan, designated by the premier as first chairman of the Board of Governors. McEwan was recommended by William Stewart, the minister of agriculture, and Everett Biggs, his deputy, because of his youth (he was then 38) and community contributions that included the organization of a citizens' committee for a new university.[33]

William Stewart seconded the premier's motion and in another unusual break with legislative procedure made a lengthy speech, putting on record the historical accomplishments of the Department of Agriculture's colleges and highlighting the university's agricultural mission. "The university will grow and will expand from an agricultural nucleus and an agricultural concept."[34] Stewart acknowledged that students in arts and science courses would benefit from being on the same campus with agriculture students and vice-versa, and he foresaw "an improved understanding between rural and urban students which will carry over into their positions in life ..."[35]

Speaking for the Liberal and New Democratic parties respectively, both Robert Nixon and Donald MacDonald echoed the government's optimism in welcoming the bill. Nixon agreed "that the essential agricultural nucleus" had to be preserved. MacDonald identified the importance of research and looked forward to the prospect of graduate education to the doctoral level.[36]

Even as the welcome notes reverberated, reaction to the legislation in the Legislature and in Guelph revealed considerable confusion still lingering about the nature of the university. When Premier Robarts moved second reading on May 5, Farquhar Oliver, the Liberal Leader of the Opposition, wanted to know whether staff of the University of Guelph would be civil servants under the Department of Agriculture? "Will they have the same freedom that the University of Toronto staff has?"[37] Robarts had to reassure the Opposition that "this will be a university in fact as well as in name."[38]

When the deans and faculty of OVC and OAC had a chance to read the proposed legislation, they became alarmed for different reasons. Bill 133 did not specifically mention the Guelph colleges as integral parts of the new university, apart from stating that each would be federated with the new university from July 1, 1964. Dean Jones of the Ontario Veterinary College wrote a letter of protest to the premier on May 7, raising the spectre of a loss of accreditation for his professional school if it was not specifically included in the new act.

> Though university status has been imposed on this campus, once the decision was made, my staff has looked forward to sharing in the development of a university here. They expect to receive the privileges and rights of a University faculty, and to accept the responsibilities, on an equal footing with other faculties. They will not, however, give up their standing among their professional colleagues on this continent and throughout the world ...[39]

Dean Richards of OAC protested that his college was not specifically included within the university and the Faculty Association joined the chorus with a letter to Premier Robarts. They reiterated the need to strengthen the position of agriculture within the new university by making the heads of the academic departments in OAC and OVC members of the university Senate.[40]

The government moved quickly to calm these fears. J.R. McCarthy, now the deputy minister in the Department of University Affairs, wrote to Dean Richards assuring him the government had intended all along to include the three colleges as integral elements of the university.[41] On May 7, the government amended the University of Guelph bill to specify the right of academic department heads in the three colleges to be members of Senate.[42] This placated the faculty and deans at Guelph, although there were still some in the Legislature who were puzzled by the proposed relationship between the colleges and the university. The bill was passed by the Legislature on May 8, 1964 and the University of Guelph came into being. The Board of Governors of the university had its first meeting that day under its chairman, T.A. McEwan, whose efforts to create a university had now come to fruition. Another member of the board was F.W. Presant who had helped to guide first OAC and then the Federated Colleges through the transitional years to university status.

The Board of Governors quickly clarified the relationship of the university to the government when it met together with the Board of Regents of the Federated Colleges in September to facilitate the transition. The two boards agreed unanimously,

> That the University of Guelph should be completely free of suggestion that it is a Government institution and should be treated on the same basis as other Ontario universities.[43]

The last vestige of the idea of a state university, modelled on either the western Canadian or the American examples like Cornell, disappeared. Guelph would not be the University of Ontario.

Further legislation was required to transfer property from the Department of Agriculture to the new university. When this amendment was passed in June, 1965, the aims of the university were also modified to include specifically, "the dissemination of knowledge respecting agriculture."[44]

Guelph delayed the celebration of its university status until May, 1965 when the first convocation was held. J.D. MacLachlan was formally installed as the University of Guelph's first president and former premier, George Drew, a native of Guelph, became the university's first chancellor. Graduates received their degrees from the University of Guelph instead of the University of Toronto.

The first honorary degree was awarded, appropriately, to the man acknowledged as the greatest living graduate of OAC, John Kenneth Galbraith. It was Galbraith's public criticism of his alma mater in the late 1940s that had drawn alumni and government attention to the pressing need for change. By giving the first honorary degree to Galbraith, the university implicitly recognized his contribution to the transformation that produced a university at Guelph.

Galbraith's criticisms had stirred up passionate feelings among his fellow alumni and former teachers. In presenting him for the degree, President MacLachlan used wit and humour in deftly acknowledging the incisive attack Galbraith had directed against OAC. Galbraith responded in kind. The exchange showed that his earlier denunciation had at last been forgiven if not forgotten. Galbraith revealed to the convocation audience that not everyone at Guelph had forgiven him.

He told convocation that he had been on a walk before breakfast that morning "in pursuit of a good Calvinist upbringing" and had encountered one of his old professors, still hale and hearty. The professor accosted him,

"I hear, Galbraith, that they are giving you an honorary degree."

Galbraith acknowledged this was true. The professor then snorted,

"I belong to the old school that thinks they should have taken away the one you have."[45]

The new president in his installation address laid down the guidelines for the future of the university he had worked so hard to create. Guelph was "the newest, yet among the oldest" in the province. MacLachlan promised that it "will not cast aside tradition in the pursuit of mere novelty, nor, on the other hand, will it allow the weight of years to prevent the introduction of new concepts and methods."

Looking ahead to the aims and philosophy that would characterize the university, MacLachlan stressed the balance to be achieved between the traditional roles of the founding colleges and the need to be at the forefront of change.

> The University of Guelph is not ambitious to be great in all things, but will strive for excellence in those areas and disciplines which can be enriched by the traditions of the past and by opportunities of the future. We intend to maintain our well-established reputation for research and services to agriculture and to rural society in general, to unfold new fields of endeavour; and wish to be known as a university that is fully aware of tradition, yet resilient and responsive to the demands of a new age.[46]

Erich Barth

From its beginnings in 1874, the college on the hill has been an important part of the Guelph community.

ENDNOTES

Chapter 1

1 Ontario Agricultural College, "Proceedings of the Celebration of the Seventy-Fifth Anniversary" (June 18, 1949).

2 Ontario Agricultural College, souvenir booklet published for the 75th anniversary celebrations on June 18, 1949.

3 OAC souvenir booklet, June 18, 1949.

4 K.J. Rea, *Prosperous Years: The Economic History of Ontario, 1919-1975* (Toronto: University of Toronto Press, 1985), pp. 135-150.

5 Report of the Provincial Farm Commission, dated January 31, 1874, cited in Alexander M. Ross, *The College on the Hill: A History of the Ontario Agricultural College, 1874-1974,* (Toronto: Copp Clark, 1974), p. 10.

6 Terry Crowley, "Madonnas before Magdalenes: Adelaide Hoodless and the Making of the Canadian Gibson Girl," *Canadian Historical Review,* 67, No. 4 (1986), 520-47.

7 For the early history of OAC, see Alexander M. Ross, *The College on the Hill* and Maria Kaars Sijpesteijn, "The Influence of the Educational Philosophy and Campus Planning Trends on the Evolution of the Guelph Campus," Master of Landscape Architecture thesis (University of Guelph, 1987).

8 J. K. Galbraith, "Horse and Buggy Teaching at OAC Instead of Scientific Research" and "Defence from Politics is Needed in OAC," *Saturday Night* (April 24 & May 8, 1948).

9 Dean A.C. Lewis, "Report of a Survey of the Ontario Agricultural College" (May 6, 1947), in Public Archives of Ontario (hereafter cited as PAO), R.G. 16-09, box 229.

10 Statement by W.R. Reek on June 17, 1944, in PAO, R.G. 16-09, box 236. For the OAC alumni view see "A Board of Governors for the Ontario Agricultural College" (February 2, 1937), in PAO, R.G. 16-09, box 236.

11 "Report of the College Inquiry Committee Appointed by the Minister of Agriculture" (February 9, 1945), in PAO, R.G. 16-09, box 246.

12 "Advantages of Boards of Governors at the Ontario Agricultural College and the Ontario Veterinary College" (February 12, 1945), in PAO, R.G. 16-09, box 246.

13 *Guelph Daily Mercury* (February 16 & March 13, 1945).

14 Letter from W.R. Reek to W.G. Thompson, dated February 13, 1945 and Reek to C. Snyder, dated January 13, 1945; "Draft Bill to create the Royal College of Ontario," March 15, 1945 in PAO, R.G. 16-09, box 246.

15 *Legislature of Ontario Debates* (March 1, 1961), p. 1650.

16 "Ontario Agricultural College Alumni Association Conservation Brief" (November 5, 1949), in PAO, R.G. 18, D-I-44.

17 "OACAA Conservation Brief" (November 5, 1949).

18 "OACAA Conservation Brief" (November 5, 1949).

19 "Notes on the Hearing with the OAC Alumni Association" (November 7, 1949), in PAO, R.G. 18, D-I-44.

20 "Brief Presented by the Ontario Federation of Agriculture" (December 7, 1949), in PAO, R.G. 18, D-I-44.

21 Report of the Select Committee on Conservation, dated 1950, p. 64.

22 *Toronto Daily Star* (February 1, 1950).

[23] *The Farmer's Advocate and Home Magazine* (March 9, 1950).

[24] Press release, dated August 25, 1950, in PAO, R.G. 16-09, box 229.

[25] Information received by the author in an interview with Fred Presant on November 26, 1987.

[26] Presant interview, November 26, 1987.

[27] Information received by the author in an interview with Trevor Lloyd Jones on June 17, 1987.

[28] Jones interview, June 17, 1987.

[29] Reports of the OAC Advisory Board, dated 1951 & 1953, in PAO, R.G. 16-09, boxes 229 & 231.

[30] "A Brief on the Status of the Ontario Agricultural College Advisory Board to the Hon. T.L. Kennedy, Minister of Agriculture" (December 3, 1951), in PAO, R.G. 16-09, box 229.

[31] *Saturday Night* (June 5, 1948). For information on Reginald Stratford, see *The Review*, 72 (Spring, 1988), pp. 18-19.

[32] "Statements Re Terms of Reference," comp. G.N. Ruhnke (June 4, 1953), in PAO, R.G. 16-09, box 230.

[33] "Statements," comp. Ruhnke.

[34] Minutes of the 19th OAC Advisory Board meeting on November 2, 1953, in PAO, R.G. 16-09, box 228.

[35] *The Ontarion* (November 19 & 22, 1952).

[36] Minutes of the 20th OAC Advisory Board meeting on April 1, 1954, in PAO, R.G. 16-09, box 229.

[37] Minutes of the 21st OAC Advisory Board meeting on May 7, 1954, appendix E, "Report of Committee in Respect to the Federation of the Three Existing Institutions Presently Located on the Campus at Guelph," in PAO, R.G. 16-09, box 229.

[38] "Federation of the Three Existing Institutions" (May 7, 1954).

[39] J.D. MacLachlan, "A Proposal for the Unification and Co-ordination of the Campus," attachment to minutes of the 24th OAC Advisory Board meeting on February 25, 1955, in PAO, R.G. 16-09, box 229.

[40] Memorandum by R.K. Stratford, dated September 6, 1956, in PAO, R.G. 16-09, box 229.

[41] Paul Axelrod, *Scholars and Dollars: Politics, Economics and the Universities of Ontario, 1945-1980*, (Toronto: University of Toronto Press, 1982), pp. 23-26.

[42] Personal letter from G. Gathercole to Premier Robarts, dated February 25, 1964, in PAO, MU 5352-D2-box 44.

[43] Letter from S. Smith to J.D. MacLachlan, dated February 11, 1957, in University of Guelph Archives, RE1, OAC AO 164.

[44] Information received by the author in an interview with J.D. MacLachlan on May 21, 1987.

[45] *Debates* (February 20, 1957), p. 510.

[46] *Debates* (March 11, 1957), p. 919.

[47] *Debates* (March 11, 1957), p. 937.

[48] *Debates* (March 21, 1956), p. 1322.

[49] Information received by the author in an interview with D.R. Campbell on August 6, 1987.

[50] Minutes of the 3rd conjoint meeting of the Advisory Committees for OAC, OVC and Macdonald Institute on May 28, 1957, in PAO, R.G. 16-01, box 1.

[51] *The Simcoe Reformer* (April 26, 1957).

[52] *Reformer* (April 26, 1957).

Chapter 2

[1] Minutes of the 6th OAC Advisory Committee meeting on September 16-17, 1957, in PAO, R.G. 16-09, box 236.

[2] *The Ontarion* (February 13, 1957).

[3] Minutes of the 7th OAC Advisory Committee meeting on December 9-10, 1957, in PAO, R.G. 16-01, box 27.

[4] Minutes of the 8th OAC Advisory Committee meeting on March 10, 1958, in PAO, R.G. 16-09, box 237.

[5] Letter from F.W. Presant to Hon. W.A. Goodfellow, dated March 27, 1958, in PAO, R.G. 16-01, box 35.

[6] Presant to Goodfellow, March 27, 1958.

[7] Letter from Goodfellow to W.J. Dunlop, dated May 2, 1958 and from Goodfellow to Premier L. Frost, dated May 2, 1958, in PAO, R.G. 16-01, box 35.

[8] Letter from Dunlop to Goodfellow, dated May 20, 1958, in PAO, R.G. 16-01, box 35.

[9] Letter from H. G. Gordon, Executive Assistant to Premier Frost, to Goodfellow, dated May 7, 1958, in PAO, R.G. 16-01, box 35.

[10] Letter from Presant to Goodfellow, dated June 18, 1958, with enclosure "Report to the minister of agriculture from the Advisory Board for Conjoint Administration," in PAO, R.G. 16-01, box 35.

[11] Minutes of meeting on September 25, 1958, in PAO, R.G. 16-01, box 35.

[12] Letter from R.A. Farrell to Goodfellow, October 22, 1958, in PAO, R.G. 16-01, box 35.

[13] J.D. MacLachlan, "Government and Administration of the Proposed University" (September 1958) and "Some Recommendations for Consideration" (n.d.), in University of Guelph Archives, RE 1, OAC A0 164.

[14] "A University on the Guelph Campus — Proposals submitted by the Advisory Board for the Ontario Agricultural College, Ontario Veterinary College and Macdonald Institute" (February 13, 1959), in PAO, R.G. 16-01, box 35.

[15] "Resumé of discussion relative to raising the status of the Ontario Agricultural College, Ontario Veterinary College and Macdonald Institute to the status of a Provincial University held in the office of the Minister of Agriculture on February 13, 1959," in PAO, R.G. 16-01, box 35.

[16] Confidential memorandum from Farrell to Goodfellow, dated February 23, 1959, in PAO, R.G. 16-01, box 35.

[17] A. D. Hales to Goodfellow, February 10, 1959, in PAO, R.G. 16-01, box 35.

[18] Minutes of the 7th conjoint meeting of the Advisory Committees for OAC, OVC and Macdonald Institute on November 30, 1959, in PAO, R.G. 16-01, box 1.

[19] Minutes of 7th conjoint meeting of the Advisory Committees for OAC, OVC and Macdonald Institute on November 30, 1959.

[20] *Guelph Daily Mercury* (August 26, 1959).

[21] "Reorganization of the Guelph Campus as a University" (1959), and "An Act Respecting a University at Guelph" (October, 1959), in PAO, R.G. 16-01, box 35.

[22] "A University on the Guelph Campus" (November 1, 1959), in PAO, R.G. 16-01, box 35.

[23] Axelrod, *Scholars and Dollars,* pp. 89-92.

[24] Minutes of 7th conjoint meeting of the Advisory Committees for OAC, OVC and Macdonald Institute on November 30, 1959.

[25] *Windsor Star* (November 27, 1959).

[26] Information received by the author in an interview with J.R. McCarthy on July 7, 1987.

[27] Rough notes of meeting on November 13, 1959, in PAO, R.G. 32, box 42.

[28] Letter from Gathercole to Frost, dated December 1, 1959, on the subject of "the Future of the Ontario Agricultural College," in PAO, R.G. 16-01, box 35.

[29] Gathercole to Frost, December 1, 1959.

[30] Gathercole to Frost, December 1, 1959.

[31] *London Free Press* (December 3, 1959).

[32] Letter from MacLachlan to Goodfellow, dated December 4, 1959, in PAO, R.G. 16-01, box 35.

[33] Information received by the author in an interview with J.R. McCarthy on July 7, 1987.

[34] MacLachlan interview, May 28, 1987.

[35] Jones interview, June 17, 1987.

Chapter 3

[1] Woods Gordon study, dated May 13, 1960, in PAO, R.G. 16-01, box 36.

[2] Letter from MacLachlan to Goodfellow, dated February 29, 1960.

[3] Information received by the author in an interview with J.D. MacLachlan on May 28, 1987.

[4] Campbell interview, August 6, 1987.

[5] *Guelph Daily Mercury* (March 31, 1960).

[6] Letter from MacLachlan to Goodfellow, dated February 29, 1960, in PAO, R.G. 16-01, box 36.

[7] Minutes of Advisory Committee on University Affairs meetings on June 3, June 9, August 4 and September 15, 1960, in PAO, George Gathercole Papers, MU 5358, series D-3, box 50.

[8] Letter from MacLachlan to Goodfellow, dated July 28, 1960, with enclosure, "An Act Respecting The Federated Colleges at Guelph," in PAO, R.G. 16-01, box 36.

[9] Personal letter from Goodfellow to Frost, dated August 16, 1960, in PAO R.G. 16-01, box 36.

[10] Letter from Presant to Goodfellow, dated January 6, 1961, in PAO, R.G. 16-01, box 36.

[11] Letter from C.W. Caskey to Goodfellow, dated January 23, 1961, in PAO, R.G. 16-01, box 36.

[12] Letter from Frost to H.A. Cotnam, dated March 7, 1961, in PAO, R.G. 32, box 2.

[13] Frost to Cotnam, March 7, 1961.

[14] Frost to Cotnam, March 7, 1961.

[15] McCarthy interview, July 7, 1987.

[16] Personal letter from Goodfellow to Frost, dated May 31, 1961, in PAO, R.G. 16-01, box 36.

[17] Letter from Frost to Goodfellow, dated June 28, 1961, in PAO, R.G. 16-01, box 36.

[18] *The Rural Co-operator* (July 18, 1961).

[19] *The Rural Co-operator* (November 29, 1960).

[20] Campbell interview, August 6, 1987.

[21] *The Ontarion* (November 30, 1960).

[22] *The Rural Co-operator* (November 29, 1960).

[23] Jim White column in *The Ontarion* (March 1, 1961).

[24] Letter from W. Newman to Goodfellow, dated November 15, 1960, in PAO, R.G. 16-01, box 36.

[25] *Debates* (March 1, 1961), p. 1650.

[26] Campbell interview, August 6, 1987.

[27] D.R. Campbell, "OAC at the Crossroads" (June 28, 1961), in PAO, R. G. 16-01, box 27.

[28] Campbell, "Crossroads."

[29] Campbell, "Crossroads."

[30] Campbell interview, August 6, 1987.

[31] Information received by the author in an interview with W.A. Stewart on February 4, 1988.

[32] *Debates* (November 22, 1961), p. 4.

[33] "Supplement to Bill 49 and Bill 50" (n.d.), in PAO, R.G. 16-01, box 183.

[34] *Debates* (March 6, 1962), p. 891.

[35] Minutes of Standing Committee on Agriculture meetings on February 28 and March 20, 1962, in PAO, R.G. 18, box 1.

[36] Letter from G. Greenlees to E. Biggs, dated March 5, 1962, in PAO, R.G. 16-09, box 185.

[37] Greenlees to Biggs, March 5, 1962.

[38] *The Ontarion* (September 26, 1962).

[39] *Guelph Daily Mercury* (September 26, 1962).

[40] Letter from Caskey to Biggs, dated October 26, 1962, in PAO, R.G. 16-09, box 185.

[41] Letter from Biggs to W. Stewart, dated October 4, 1962, in PAO, R. G. 16-09, box 251.

Chapter 4

[1] On the background to the changes in higher education, see Blair Neatby "Communities of Scholars in Ontario," in Cicely Watson (ed) *The Professoriate: Occupation in Crisis* (Toronto: Ontario Institute for Studies in Education, 1985), pp. 10-28.

[2] R. Jackson, "Survey of Secondary School Enrolment and University Full-time Undergraduate Enrolment, with Projections of University Enrolment to 1971-72" (March, 1962), in PAO, R.G. 32, box 2.

[3] Letter from R.B. Jackson to F.S. Rivers, dated March 26, 1962, in PAO, R.G. 32, box 60.

[4] Minutes of Advisory Committee on University Affairs meeting on May 29, 1961, in PAO, George Gathercole Papers, MU 5338, series D3, box 50.

[5] Minutes of Advisory Committee on University Affairs meeting on June 26, 1961, in PAO, George Gathercole Papers, MU 5338, series D3, box 50.

6 Axelrod, *Scholars and Dollars* p. 92. For his assessment of the Committee's place in the province's higher education policy between 1958 and 1967, see pp. 89-99.

7 Letter from C. Bissell to Frost, dated May 17, 1962, with enclosure, "Report on Post-Secondary Education in Ontario, 1962-1970." This report was revised in January, 1963 and published as *Post-Secondary Education in Ontario, 1962-1970.*

8 *Post-Secondary Education in Ontario,* p. 3.

9 *Post-Secondary Education in Ontario,* p. 24.

10 Agenda of meeting on July 19, 1962, in PAO, R.G. 32, box 6.

11 Document presented by Col. E.W. Phillips to Advisory Committee on December 11, 1962, in PAO, R.G. 32, box 6.

12 Phillips to Advisory Committee, December 11, 1962.

13 Minutes of Advisory Committee on University Affairs meeting on January 16, 1962, in PAO, R.G. 32, box 42.

14 Minutes of Advisory Committee on University Affairs meeting on January 8, 1963, in PAO, R.G. 32, box 42.

15 University Affairs minutes, January 8, 1963.

16 University Affairs minutes, January 8, 1963.

17 *Debates* (February 27, 1963), pp. 1146-7.

18 *Debates* (February 27, 1963), pp. 1146-7.

19 Axelrod, *Scholars and Dollars,* pp. 54-76.

20 Information received by the author in an interview with T.A. McEwan on July 20, 1987.

21 McEwan interview, July 20, 1987.

22 Report from A. Hagar to W.C. Winegard, dated September, 1967, entitled "The Guelph Citizens' Committee and the formation of the University of Guelph," in Aubrey Hagar Papers.

23 Information received by the author in an interview with A. Hagar on August 4, 1987.

24 Letter from T.A. McEwan to the author, dated October 11, 1988.

25 McEwan to the author, October 11, 1988.

26 Letter from McEwan to MacLachlan, dated December 3, 1962, in Aubrey Hagar Papers.

27 McEwan to MacLachlan, December 3, 1962.

28 Letter from MacLachlan to McEwan, dated December 12, 1962, in University of Guelph Archives, RE1, FED, AO28.

29 Hagar, "Guelph Citizens' Committee," September 1967.

30 Letter, from D.A. Barnum to the author, dated January 2, 1989.

31 Information received by the author in an interview with J.W. Gilman on January 20, 1989.

32 "The Need for Increased University Facilities and the Federated Colleges" (Copy No. 9, n.d.), in Aubrey Hagar Papers.

33 "Increased University Facilities," (Copy No. 9, n.d.)

34 A. Hagar, "Suggestions for brief on University Status" (January 25, 1963), in Aubrey Hagar Papers.

35 Letter from McEwan to Robarts, dated February 11, 1963, in Aubrey Hagar Papers.

36 McEwan to Robarts, February 11, 1963.

37 Letter from MacLachlan to Hagar, dated February 15, 1963, in Aubrey Hagar Papers, and confidential letter from MacLachlan to Biggs, February 15, 1963, in PAO, R.G. 16-09, box 251.

38 Letter from Robarts to McEwan, dated February 14, 1963, in Aubrey Hagar Papers.

39 Hagar, "The Guelph Citizens' Committee," September 1967.

40 *Debates* (February 27, 1963), p. 1147.

41 *The Globe and Mail* (March 6, 1963).

42 *Guelph Daily Mercury* (March 12, 1963).

43 *The Ontarion* (March 14, 1963).

44 *The Ontarion* (March 14, 1963).

45 Minutes of Advisory Committee on University Affairs meeting on March 28, 1963, in PAO, R.G. 32, box 42.

[46] University Affairs minutes, March 28, 1963.

[47] Letter from M.A. Tovell to Presant, dated April 26, 1963, in Aubrey Hagar Papers.

[48] Letter from Presant to Tovell, dated May 2, 1963, in Aubrey Hagar Papers.

[49] Letter from McEwan to Robarts, dated May 14, 1963, in Aubrey Hagar Papers.

[50] Minutes of Advisory Committee on University Affairs meeting on May 15, 1963, in PAO, R.G. 32, box 42.

[51] Minutes of 4th Board of Regents meeting on March 11-12, 1963, in PAO, R.G. 16-09, box 232.

[52] "An Appraisal of the Guelph Campus for Development as a University" (March 27, 1963), in PAO, R.G. 16-09, box 251.

[53] "Guelph Campus for Development" (March 27, 1963).

[54] Minutes of 5th Board of Regents meeting on June 10-11, 1963, in PAO, R.G. 16-09, box 232.

[55] Reports by Deans Richards and Jones, dated July, 1963, in University of Guelph Archives, REI, FED, A058.

[56] J.D. MacLachlan, "Proposed Organizational Structure for the University of the Guelph Campus" (August 20, 1963), confidential report, in PAO, R.G. 16-09, box 251.

[57] J.D. MacLachlan, "Comments on Choices for the Organizational Design of a University on the Guelph Campus" (August, 1963), in PAO, R.G. 16-02, box 57.

[58] MacLachlan, "Proposed Organizational Structure" (August 20, 1963). See also text of remarks for J.D. MacLachlan's presentation to Board of Regents on February 3, 1964, entitled "Review of Events," in PAO, R.G. 16-09, box 232.

[59] MacLachlan, "Proposed Organizational Structure" (August 20, 1963).

Chapter 5

[1] Remarks from MacLachlan's presentation to Board of Regents, February 3, 1964.

[2] Stewart interview, February 4, 1988.

[3] Stewart interview, February 4, 1988.

[4] Report from Biggs to W.A. Stewart, "Relationship of the Present Three Colleges to the New University" (October 15, 1963), in PAO, R.G. 16-09, box 251.

[5] "Relationship of the Present Three Colleges" (October 15, 1963).

[6] Biggs, "Proposed Steps in University Organization on Guelph Campus" (October 15, 1963), in PAO, R.G. 16-09, box 251.

[7] J.R. McCarthy, "University of Guelph" (October 21, 1963); "The Question of University Government" (October 18, 1963); "Some Advantages of a Government University at Guelph" (October 18, 1963), in PAO, R.G. 16-09, box 251.

[8] McCarthy, "U of G;" "The Question;" "Government University."

[9] McCarthy, "U of G;" "The Question;" "Government University."

[10] McCarthy, "U of G;" "The Question;" "Government University."

[11] McCarthy, "U of G;" "The Question;" "Government University."

[12] Minutes of Advisory Committee for University Affairs meeting on October 30, 1963, in PAO, R.G. 32, box 42.

[13] Stewart interview, February 4, 1988.

[14] *The Ontarion* (October 3, 1963).

[15] Letter from J.G.F. Morton to Biggs, dated May 8, 1963, enclosing report of the University Government Committee, dated April 29, 1963, in PAO, R.G. 16-09, box 251.

[16] Morton to Biggs, May 8, 1963.

[17] Memorandum from J.R. Stevens to the author, dated January 17, 1989.

[18] Stevens to author, January 17, 1989.

[19] Letter from J.P.W. Gilman to Stewart, dated February 4, 1964, enclosing brief entitled "Matters concerning the Proposed Establishment of a University at Guelph," in PAO, R.G. 16-02, box 57.

[20] Gilman to Stewart, February 4, 1964.

[21] Gilman to Stewart, February 4, 1964.

[22] Letter from Gilman to the author, dated January 23, 1989.

[23] Letter from R.A. Stewart to W.A. Stewart, dated January 1, 1964; minutes of OAC Alumni Association meeting with W.A. Stewart on January 8, 1964, in PAO, R.G. 16-02, box 57.

[24] Minutes of Advisory Committee on University Affairs meeting on January 7, 1964, in PAO, R.G. 32, box 42.

[25] MacLachlan interview, May 28, 1987; remarks from MacLachlan's presentation to the Board of Regents, February 3, 1964.

[26] MacLachlan interview, May 28, 1987; remarks from MacLachlan's presentation to the Board of Regents, February 3, 1964.

[27] *The Ontarion* (January 23, 1964).

[28] Stewart interview, February 4, 1988.

[29] *Debates* (April 24, 1964), p. 2441.

[30] *Debates* (April 24, 1964), p. 2442.

[31] MacLachlan interview, May 28, 1987.

[32] MacLachlan interview, May 28, 1987.

[33] Letter from Biggs to W.A. Stewart, dated January 6, 1964, in PAO, R.G. 16-09, box 251.

[34] *Debates* (April 24, 1964), pp. 2443-2445.

[35] *Debates* (April 24, 1964), pp. 2443-2445.

[36] *Debates* (April 24, 1964), pp. 2443-2445.

[37] *Debates* (May 5, 1964), p. 2838.

[38] *Debates* (May 5, 1964), p. 2838.

[39] Letter from Jones to Premier Robarts, dated May 7, 1964, in PAO, R.G. 16-09, box 251; telegram from Jones to Biggs, dated May 1, 1964, in PAO, R.G. 16-09, box 251.

[40] Letter from N.R. Richards to Biggs, dated May 5, 1964, in PAO, R.G. 16-09, box 251; Letter from Gilman to Premier Robarts, dated May 1, 1964, in PAO, R.G. 16-09, box 251.

[41] Letter from McCarthy to Richards, dated May 8, 1964, in University of Guelph Archives, REI, FED, AO45.

[42] *Debates* (May 7, 1964), p. 2931.

[43] Letter from McEwan to W.A. Stewart, dated September 9, 1964, in PAO, R.G. 16-09, box 251.

[44] Statutes of Ontario, *The University of Guelph Amendment Act, 1965*, Chapter 136.

[45] J.K. Galbraith, Convocation Address, delivered on May 21, 1965, recording in University of Guelph Archives.

[46] MacLachlan, Convocation Address, May 21, 1965.